MW01129767

Navigating Uncertainty

Navigating Uncertainty

Sensemaking for Educational Leaders

By

Shelley Hasinoff
David Mandzuk

BRILL

SENSE

LEIDEN | BOSTON

All chapters in this book have undergone peer review.

The Library of Congress Cataloging-in-Publication Data is available online at http://catalog.loc.gov

Typeface for the Latin, Greek, and Cyrillic scripts: "Brill". See and download: brill.com/brill-typeface.

ISBN 978-90-04-36847-7 (paperback)
ISBN 978-90-04-36846-0 (hardback)
ISBN 978-90-04-36848-4 (e-book)

Contents

Figures and Tables

Figures

Tables

Introduction

Although we had already been working on this book for over a year, the actual writing began in earnest in the summer of 2016. We recall this as a time of rampant uncertainty. In fact, pundits began to refer to this period as the beginning of the "post-truth" era. In North America, this state of affairs was exacerbated by the US presidential election campaign in which the often wild and contra-factual allegations by the Republican candidate, Donald Trump, seemed to dominate every news cycle. The issue of what is true, whose truth matters, and whether voters could continue to have confidence in the election process itself frustrated any attempt to focus on the real issues. The proliferation of so-called fake news reports and increasing evidence that the Russian government had interfered in the election campaign simply added to the uncertainty. Moreover, global concerns, including the Syrian refugee crisis, the so-called "Brexit," catastrophic climatic events, militaristic threats from North Korea, and the all-too-frequent attacks against innocent civilians, including school children, contributed to a pervasive sense of unease and increased divisiveness, often along political party lines.

In such turbulent times, trust in our institutions and systems and trust in members of our social networks is severely strained. Ironically, however, just when our beliefs in institutions and the people tasked with administering them are diminished, educational leaders are being entrusted to take on ever more expanding responsibilities. Educational leaders, for example, are expected to be experts in their field, excellent managers of physical plants, insightful problem solvers, skilled brokers between educational institutions and communities, highly capable stewards of staff development, and visionaries who are able to guide their institutions masterfully through difficult financial times. Above all, educational leaders are expected to build and sustain trusting relationships in their social networks. Indeed, such relationships are critical for our success as educational leaders because we cannot hope to work towards common goals or create the optimal conditions for teaching and learning without them.

Unfortunately, few educational leaders have had sufficient training in how to nurture relationships or how to repair them when they break down. This is due, in part, to the myth that such "soft" skills do not need to be taught and deep-seated beliefs that when it comes to leading, "experience is the best teacher." We argue, on the contrary, that such skills are far from being intuitive and that educational leaders need specific guidance to explore, understand, make sense of, and respond to uncertainty and the complex problems and crises that arise from it. To address this gap, we developed the 5-step sensemaking approach, which we introduce and model through scenarios drawn from interviews with educational leaders and our own experiences as administrators.

Prior to writing the book, we asked 15 superintendents, deans, and principals to use the 5-step sensemaking approach to share a complex problem or dilemma with our research assistant, who transcribed the sessions. Although the scenarios are set in particular milieus, they reflect the kinds of dilemmas that occur in any setting. To maximize the impact of the scenarios, we recommend that readers focus on the challenges being portrayed rather than the fact that the setting may be different than their own. In addition to the scenarios, which were fictionalized to preserve anonymity, the transcriptions were mined for illustrative quotes that are interspersed throughout the book and are identified only by the role of the person speaking. A brief description of the chapters is included below.

In Chapter 1, *Exploring Uncertainty*, we make the case that uncertainty is neither positive nor negative, but is, instead, an inescapable characteristic of the complex adaptive systems in which we work. In this context, we examine warranted and unwarranted certainties and uncertainties as important touchstones for educational leaders. We introduce the *Certainty Matrix* as a tool to help educational leaders think about what they know and how they know it. Finally, we present a scenario which illustrates the overlapping concerns of educational leaders at different levels of a complex adaptive educational system.

In Chapter 2, *Understanding Uncertainty*, we focus on the dilemmas and crises that educational leaders inevitably face in complex adaptive systems. This leads us to consider complexity leadership theory and social capital as resources that can help educational leaders come to a deeper understanding of uncertainty. We show how the three roles of complexity leadership (administrative, enabling, and adaptive) relate to three key sources of social capital (norms, networks, and trust). Finally, we present a scenario that illustrates the importance of social capital in educational leadership.

In Chapter 3, *Making Sense of Uncertainty*, we describe the 5-step sensemaking approach in detail. Rooted in sensemaking, this approach engages readers in an iterative series of guided questions, completing a Certainty Matrix, and creating a relationship map to make sense of what happened in order to formulate a course of action. Educational leaders who have used this approach say that they are able to reach a deeper understanding of difficult challenges and the roles they played in them. At the end of the chapter, we model the 5-step sensemaking approach with a scenario that illustrates how an educational leader makes sense of the complex relationships in her workplace.

In Chapter 4, *Grappling with Uncertainty*, we provide three scenarios from three different settings. We follow three educational leaders as they use the 5-step sensemaking approach to respond to the challenges they face and consider the courses of action open to them.

In Chapter 5, *Responding to Cases of Uncertainty*, we present 9 scenarios for educational leaders to practice applying the 5-step sensemaking approach on their own.

Who the Book Is For

This book was written for educational leaders who are currently leading educational institutions as well as those who are considering a career in educational administration, regardless of the educational setting in which they find themselves.

Acknowledgements

We would like to thank the following superintendents, principals, deans who freely and generously participated in the interviews and preliminary testing of the 5- step sensemaking approach. They are listed alphabetically as follows: Airini, Sal Badali, Gwen Birse, Mike Borgfjord, Cathy Bruce, Dionne Deer, Randy Dueck, Heather Duncan, Mark den Hollander, Vinh Huynh, Barb Isaak, Rod Kehler, Vern Reimer, Jennifer Tupper, and Leslie Wurtak. We would also like to thank our colleagues, friends, and family for their suggestions and support during this project. Finally, we would like to acknowledge the important contributions of Catherine Draper who conducted and transcribed the interviews and provided us with valuable insights throughout the course of the project.

CHAPTER 1

Exploring Uncertainty

> School communities face a complex landscape of challenges where uncertainty has become the norm. Difficult policy climates, failed school improvement, the scarcity of financial resources, violence, tragedy, poverty, and maintaining a quality teacher workforce are among the social and professional issues school leaders are expected to navigate while building meaningful communities of learning.
>
> SUTHERLAND, "Learning and growing: Trust, leadership, and response to crisis," *Journal of Educational Administration*, 2017, p. 2

∴

Uncertainty has been defined as the inability "to make sense of, assign value to, or predict outcomes of events" (Kosenko, 2014, p. 1425). Uncertainty, stemming from too little or too much information can make us, as educational leaders, "lose our cool" and complicate our decision-making. Unfortunately, uncertainty is an inescapable feature of our educational systems. It can affect everything from our daily routines to our deep-seated beliefs and everything in between. While we may feel fairly certain about some things in the short-term, it takes the smallest perturbation of the system to set off a chain of events that can upend our so-called ordered existence. Consequently, we tend to associate uncertainty with discomfort and risk. However, it is important to remind ourselves that uncertainty is neither intrinsically positive nor inherently negative. Indeed, according to Dewey (1933), "the origin of thinking is some perplexity, confusion, or doubt" (p. 15).

It is telling that a military acronym VUCA (volatility, uncertainty, complexity, ambiguity) has been widely adopted by institutions, businesses, and organizations to capture the notion that disruption is not only an expected feature of organizational life but also presents unexpected opportunities (Bennett & Lemoine, 2014). We make the case that educational leaders need to understand both the risks and the benefits of working in a VUCA environment. Such environments are best described as *complex adaptive systems*.

© KONINKLIJKE BRILL NV, LEIDEN, 2018 | DOI 10.1163/9789004368484_001

1   **Complex Adaptive Systems**

Until recently, educational leaders were encouraged to lead their institutions according to the same scientific management principles that served factories and other simple organizations so well during the industrial era. Montuori (2013) argues that such principles owe much to the philosophy of Descartes (1701/1954) who wrote,

> If we are to understand a problem perfectly, we must free it from superfluous conceptions, reduce it to the simplest terms, and by process of enumerations, split it up into the smallest possible parts. (p. 179)

The rationalist thinking of Descartes and his followers helps us understand and organize complicated systems, such as assembly lines, which require standardized inputs and replicable outputs. Even extremely complicated processes, such as those involved in launching a rocket, can be replicated by developing a rigid set of protocols. However, such linear thinking fails utterly to account for how systems work as a whole or how we can accommodate uncertainty in our planning. Unlike complicated systems which can be taken apart and reassembled in exactly the same manner, complex systems, like Humpty Dumpty, cannot be put back together again (Davis & Sumara, 2005). In other words, we cannot explain complex systems by simply examining their parts.

Examples of complex systems include stock markets, human bodies, organs and cells, trees, and schools. Characteristically, complex systems resist our most strenuous efforts to achieve the same outcomes by using the same procedures. In fact, it can be counterproductive to do so. As educational leaders, we have all discovered to our chagrin that the same policy can be interpreted differently, even when our colleagues agree with it. Over time, we may even discover that the implementation of a policy has resulted in unintended negative consequences and we may be forced to formulate yet another policy in order to bring the system back into balance. What worked in the past cannot be relied upon to meet rapidly changing conditions. Who would have thought, for example, that some schools would not only be allowing students to use cell phones in the classroom, but are now relying on them to supplement existing technology?

Increasingly, educational leaders, like those in business and economic institutions, are embracing complexity theories, such as complex adaptive systems theory and complexity leadership theory because we,

...no longer see systems as complicated and principally predictable, with answers to problems which can be correct with some degree of probability, given sufficient information is available. Instead, complex systems are characterized by irreducible uncertainty and scientists can arrive at possibly correct answers, at best. In a complexity setting, 'being correct' changes its value. When decisions directly affect people's lives and their survival, being roughly right is better than being precisely wrong. (Pelc, 2017, p. 22)

Complex adaptive systems were originally developed in the biological and ecological sciences to account for non-linear adaptive behaviours in response to change. Mitleton-Kelly (2003) helps us to visualize the "intricate intertwining or inter-connectivity of elements within a system and between a system and its environment" (p. 4). She points out that the English word *complexity* is derived from the Latin word "plexus" which means braided or entwined and its derivative "complexus" which means braided together. A *system* is composed of interdependent components. A *complex system* is made up of many, dynamic, and diverse components which can interact unpredictably. The components of a complex adaptive system are able to change their behaviour in response to each other and to adapt to an ever-changing environment. Depending on the extent to which these changes from the external or internal environment threaten the survival of the system, adaptations may be modest or may change the system utterly. Indeed some adaptations may even change the environment itself.

Since complex adaptive systems are not centrally controlled, the tensions between order and chaos are managed through *self-organization* and *emergence*. Self-organization refers to "grass-roots leadership" which is taken on by agents or components to reduce chaos and return the system to equilibrium. Emergence is defined as the "arising of novel and coherent structures, patterns, and properties during the process of self-organization in complex systems" (Goldstein, 1999, p. 49). In educational settings, professional learning communities and less formal communities of practice represent attempts to foster self-organization and encourage emergence.

In both physical and social spaces, complex adaptive systems "exhibit the fundamental principles of complexity, adaptability, emergence and tension between chaos and order" (Shaked & Schechter, 2017, p. 30). Such systems cycle recursively through *disequilibrium, adaptation, equilibrium,* and *action* as illustrated in Figure 1.1 below. The use of double-pointed arrows between the processes of complex adaptive systems is meant to indicate that interactions

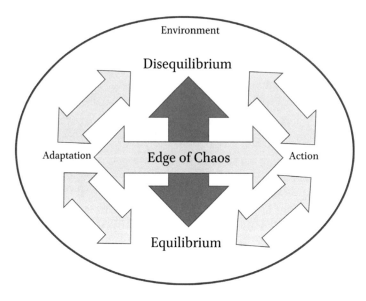

FIGURE 1.1   *Complex adaptive systems model*

take place between all of the components of complex systems and their environments and that there is no starting or ending point.

2   Equilibrium, Disequilibrium, and the Edge of Chaos

As educational leaders, we may find ourselves in an environment characterized by equilibrium, disequilibrium, or one that is close to the *edge of chaos*. A system is said to be in equilibrium when order and balance prevail. Nevertheless, "If the system settles into harmony and equilibrium, it will eventually stagnate and die" (Kelly, 1998, p. 110). Pascale et al. (2000) assert that "over time and on very large scales, equilibrium becomes hazardous. It dulls an organization's senses and saps its abilities to cope with danger" (p. 2). Furthermore, in a moribund system, even small changes can have a disproportionately large impact. The system's goal is to survive, adapt, evolve and maximize its capabilities through on-going realignment (Blandin, 2008, p. 13). Although complex adaptive systems try to preserve the status quo, unpredictable internal and external changes cause them to oscillate between equilibrium and disequilibrium, between order and chaos, and between stability and instability. As Montouri (2013) explains,

> ...every living system is both open and closed, again one of those paradoxical, both/and relationships. Open systems tend to be far

less stable than closed systems, which are by definition systems in equilibrium, with no exchange with their environment. The openness of the system leads to potential disequilibrium. Open systems are stabilized by flow, but their structural stability is only relative because this structure is gradually, and sometimes quite rapidly, transformed by exchanges with the environment. (pp. 206–207)

From an educational leader's standpoint, it might appear that disequilibrium is something we should try to avoid completely or at least make an effort to reduce as much as possible. While it is true that too much upheaval can overwhelm our ability to adapt, a certain amount of disequilibrium is necessary for a system to grow and renew itself. Indeed, the poetically named edge of chaos or "that point between linear predictability and complete chaos while still being ordered" represents the place where "a system is at its most creative, imaginative and adaptable" (Morrison, 2010, p. 377). Educational leaders who understand educational institutions to be complex adaptive systems are more likely to perceive the edge of chaos as "the sweet spot for productive change" (Pascale et al., 2000, p. 61) in which they can "expand their opportunities by creating new connections, and disrupting existing patterns of interaction" (Shaked & Schechter, 2017, p. 30).

I think that every challenging situation I encounter shapes me as a leader. (Dean)

Disequilibrium that is generated from "outside" educational institutions pervades every aspect of teaching, learning, and administration in schools, district offices, and faculties of education. External sources of uncertainty are both context specific and more broadly situated in cultural, socio-economic, and political conditions. Educational leaders, for example, must be attuned to the larger context of fiscal restraint, changing demographics, increasing political support for private and home schools, and ambivalent support for public institutions. Yet they must remain focused on fulfilling the needs of their own organizations. In some jurisdictions, the sudden influx of immigrants and refugees from diverse cultures injects uncertainty about how to use existing resources to accommodate learners for whom English is an additional language and for those whose schooling has been interrupted or was simply unavailable. Changing initiatives concerning accountability that are either mandated or incentivised by federal, provincial, or state grants leave many educational leaders wondering whether compliance or resistance is in the best interests of teachers and students. Differences among community members about what constitutes a good education also contribute to the general climate of uncertainty. While some parents, for example, may support greater technology and curriculum integration, others may want to put the brakes on change and increase the focus on "the basics."

Disequilibrium is also generated from "inside" educational settings by the individuals within them, the history of the institution, and the inherent and conflicting tensions that underlie organizational life. It is a truism of any organization that "5% of the people cause 95%" of the dilemmas. Many of us can point to situations in which one person has caused such a breakdown in trust that the equilibrium of an entire organization is threatened. As educational leaders, we may feel uncertain about our own capacity to lead, especially when we compare ourselves to leaders we admire, most of whom appear, at least from the outside, to be models of self-confidence and self-assurance (Lortie, 1975).

The longer I've been an educational leader, the more I realize how much I still need to learn about organizational life. (Principal)

An institution's history of successes and failures, including the scars of past injustices, marginalization, and preferential treatment of special interests can simmer just below the surface, affecting the way that staff members respond to the actions of their educational leader and representatives of the community. Furthermore, the often conflicting and unresolvable expectations of the leadership role can create undermining self-doubt. For example, educational leaders are simultaneously expected to maintain the status quo while embracing rapid change, be team players but think independently, lead authoritatively yet consult widely, be ever mindful of costs but ensure continued high quality, and make humane exceptions on a case by case basis yet maintain the fairness and integrity of policies meant for all. Grint (2005) refers to such contradictions as the "irony of leadership" whereas Handy (1994) uses the word "paradox" to describe the "inevitable, endemic, and perpetual" oppositional tensions of organizational life. Oppositional tensions, such as paradoxes and dilemmas which have no right or wrong solutions are often responsible for "keeping us up at night, lengthening our work hours and shortening our times of rest" (Duignan, 2003, p. 4).

Some of the difficulty we experience with the inherent tensions of leadership is that we tend to view tensions as polar opposites, from which we must choose "either/or" instead of taking a "both/and" approach in which we try to connect and understand the complementary and inseparable parts of each duality (Smith, Lewis, & Tushman, 2016). The benefits of the latter, as Ansell and Boin (2017) point out are that,

[b]y avoiding the temptation to accept simplifying definitions of a situation, one also escapes from the apparent logic of action that comes with such definitions ("now or never," "do or don't"). This principle guides decision makers toward unpacking a dilemma in processual, relational terms – seeing scales rather than categories; gray zones rather than hard boundaries – which, in turn, allows for a piecemeal approach. (p. 11)

Consider the duality of certainty and uncertainty. While certainty appears to be a laudable goal, paradoxically, certainty is often the source of uncertainty. As educational leaders, many of us think that we should have all the answers or at least know where to get them quickly. However, Senge (1995) warns us that there is a downside to being certain,

When top managers describe reality – what they perceive as reality – with an air of certainty and authority, they create an incredible mantle of ineffectiveness, because everyone then looks up to them to solve the problems, to do the thinking.

Furthermore, we may "feel" just as confident when our certainty is warranted as when it is unwarranted. Warranted certainties are based on empirical knowledge, evidence-based conclusions, and verifiable facts, whereas unwarranted certainties are grounded in unexamined assumptions, taken-for-granted beliefs, and unsupported theories. Unfortunately, as Kahneman (2011) points out, it is often our *unwarranted certainties* which are rewarded,

Experts who acknowledge the full extent of their ignorance may expect to be replaced by more confident competitors, who are better able to gain the trust of clients. An unbiased appreciation of uncertainty is a cornerstone of rationality – but it is not what people and organizations want. Extreme uncertainty is paralyzing under dangerous circumstances, and the admission that one is merely guessing is especially unacceptable when the stakes are high. Acting on pretended knowledge is often the preferred solution. (p. 263)

3   Certainty Matrix

Certainty can play a positive role in building a climate of trust or a negative role by shutting down debate. This makes it important for educational leaders to think about whether our decisions are based on warranted or unwarranted certainties or uncertainties. After all, as Fullan (2008) points out, "probably the two greatest failures of leaders are indecisiveness in times of urgent need for action and dead certainty that they are right in times of complexity" (p. 6). We created the Certainty Matrix below (Table 1.1) to help educational leaders think about what they know and how they know it.

TABLE 1.1   *Certainty Matrix (adapted from Hasinoff & Mandzuk, 2015)*

	Certainties	**Uncertainties**
Warranted	*I know, on the basis of:* – verifiable facts – peer-reviewed empirical research – evidence-based conclusions	*I don't know, due to:* – insufficient data – unverified or anecdotal evidence – lack of related knowledge or skills
Unwarranted	*I think I know, based on:* – taken-for-granted beliefs – assumptions – unsupported theories	*I ought to know, but don't due to:* – weak network ties – unclear norms – absent or tenuous trust

- *Warranted certainties*, as depicted in the upper left quadrant, arise when we can verify knowledge. Such knowledge may be a basic fact, such as the capital of France or it may be the thoughtful, replicable results of well-designed research, such as, the finding that specific descriptive feedback has a positive effect on student achievement. Certainties that are warranted are less often found in any area in which human emotions, relationships, and beliefs are involved.
- *Unwarranted certainties,* found in the lower left quadrant, arise when what we "know" is not actually supported by evidence. This kind of certainty is sometimes referred to as a "gut feeling" which, when analyzed more deeply, has little basis in fact. Unwarranted certainties that arise from this type of knowledge are usually submerged well below the surface, often clouding our ability to think critically. Indeed, educators often take the knowledge derived from myths, bandwagons, and moral panics for granted as "givens" without ever stopping to examine whether these unwarranted certainties are appropriate guides for our actions (Hasinoff & Mandzuk, 2015).
- *Warranted uncertainties*, as summarized in the upper right quadrant, occur when what we don't know is reasonable because the facts are not

in evidence or we have either inaccurate or too little information to make a determination. Uncertainties that are warranted may arise from such unresolvable questions as, "How can schools achieve excellence and equity?" or may be the result of lack of knowledge in a particular subject or area. For example, uncertainty is warranted when a person is called upon to speak in a language they know only slightly or to perform a skill such as computer programming without ever having been taught.

– *Unwarranted uncertainties*, listed in the lower right quadrant, occur when we have limited or even non-existent *social network ties,* are unaware of the prevailing *norms* or lack clarity about them, and when we have failed to establish *trust* in our relationships with others. This type of uncertainty is mostly unwarranted because, as educational leaders, we can create closer ties in our networks, become more attuned to the norms that underpin our organizations, and focus more intentionally on building and sustaining trust in our workplaces. By paying attention to network ties, transparency and stability of existing norms, and the degree of trust in relationships, educational leaders can reduce the amount of unwarranted uncertainty they need to manage and are more likely to create a positive climate in their institutions.

Often, when we are dealing with complex problems or unresolvable dilemmas, there are few warranted certainties in evidence. Indeed, most of us end up spending considerable time and energy trying to sort out and establish the "facts." Obviously, we can never know all there is to know about a situation, but we think that tools like the Certainty Matrix can go a long way toward helping us consider our own attitudes, biases, lack of knowledge, and assumptions before making decisions that we will need to justify to others.

The sad fact is that few of us can adequately explain how we arrived at some of our most difficult decisions. According to cognitive scientists, there are good evolutionary reasons for this. Human survival, after all, depends upon quick thinking in tight situations so people are hard-wired for closure. In other words, we urgently desire "any answer as long as it is definite" and then we hold on to whatever answer we have already accepted in order to avoid feeling the distress of ambiguity (Kruglanski & Webster, 1996, p. 263). In summarizing the work of Kruglanski and his colleagues on cognitive closure, Konnikova (2013) describes their conceptualization of the two major stages, seizing and freezing, as follows:

> In the first stage, we are driven by urgency, or the need to reach closure
> quickly: we "seize" whatever information we can, without necessarily

taking the time to verify it as we otherwise would. In the second stage, we are driven by permanence, or the need to preserve that closure for as long as possible: we "freeze" our knowledge and do what we can to safeguard it. (So, for instance, we support policies or arguments that validate our initial view). And once we've frozen? Our confidence increases apace.

Paradoxically, the "...more uncertain our world seems, the more we compensate by seeking out certainty" (Anastasion, 2016). Thompson (2003) puts it this way,

> Just as complete uncertainty or randomness is the antithesis of purpose and organization, complete certainty is a figment of the imagination; but the tighter the norms of rationality, the more energy the organization will devote to moving toward certainty. (p. 159)

Typically, in our quest for certainty, we direct our energies to establishing and maintaining routines rather than experiencing the discomfort and unpleasantness of not knowing (Floden & Buchmann, 1993; Floden & Clark, 1988). We may also cling tenaciously to "what works" and try to increase the predictability of our work by avoiding anything that is new or unfamiliar. To counteract such discomfort, some of us may turn to educational gurus who promise us certainty but who rarely deliver. Nevertheless, education is full of uncertainty and deep down we know "we can run, but we can't hide" from it. Every time the phone rings, there is a knock on the door, or one of our many electronic devices signals us to pay attention, we must confront uncertainty. We may find ourselves asking, "Will this be a momentary distraction or the beginning of a long descent into a rabbit hole that will take us months to climb out of?" The following scenario illustrates the kind of disequilibrium that can spread across three educational settings when a superintendent calls the dean of the nearby faculty of education.

4   Pulling the Plug

Fiona Cousins, the superintendent of a large metropolitan school district, braced herself as she began her conversation with Stan Fowler, the dean of education at one of the local universities. Stan was well known in the university community and well respected by his colleagues in the K-12 school system. Over the years, Fiona and Stan had built up a strong professional relationship and considered each other to be trusted friends. Together they had worked with the rest of the professional community to focus greater attention on teacher professionalism and the ethical aspects of teaching. However, the bombshell Fiona had just dropped made both of them wonder if their efforts had made any impact.

Fiona was calling about a teacher candidate, Rick Summerford, who was doing his practicum at Freemont High School, one of the largest high schools in her district. According to Sheila Scarth, the principal, Rick had admitted to buying cigarettes, drugs, alcohol, and movie tickets for two teenage boys at the school, both of whom were minors. Even more troubling was that there was every indication that Rick was interested sexually in at least one of the boys, if not both of them. Sheila was outraged that "this had happened on her watch" and in her words, she was ready to "pull the plug" immediately not just on Rick, but on all the teacher candidates from the faculty of education. She insisted that this incident was proof that the university was doing a poor job of screening applicants and, as a result, was placing her students in jeopardy.

Neither Fiona nor Stan knew much about Sheila, who had moved to the area a year ago with her husband and was in the first few months of her tenure as a high school principal. What they did know is that this could not have come at a worse time. The start to the school year had been rocky, to say the least, with Sheila making headlines in the local newspaper for implementing controversial decisions without sufficient parent consultation.

Given the gravity of the situation and Sheila's earlier experiences, neither Fiona nor Stan had any difficulty understanding why she was so upset. They agreed to remove the teacher candidate immediately and to bring this case to the attention of the Professional Standards Committee at the university. Given that this looked like a case of grooming, they talked about whether expulsion was an adequate response and whether the police should be involved. In any event, they agreed that removing all of the teacher candidates from the school, especially in the middle of the practicum, would do more harm than good.

Having arranged to meet with Sheila at the school the next morning, Fiona and Stan were prepared to support her and to discuss how they would address the situation as a team. However, within minutes of their arrival, Sheila was insisting that all of the teacher candidates be removed from the school at once and was threatening to go to the media and expose both the district and the university to public condemnation. As a new untenured employee, Sheila was unlikely to go ahead with her threats, but Fiona couldn't help wonder why Sheila was taking such an aggressive stand. More importantly, Fiona recognized that she not only had to diffuse the situation at hand but also that she would be dealing with its repercussions for years to come.

Although this scenario is written from the superintendent's perspective, the entire educational system, including students and parents, is affected by Rick's behaviour. The equilibrium has been disturbed and, if Sheila has her way, the entire system may well move to the edge of chaos. As the superintendent, Fiona will need to consider what actions she will take to deal with Rick's transgressions and Sheila's threats so that the system can return to equilibrium. Fiona completes the *Certainty Matrix* (Table 1.2) by summarizing the events to clarify what she is certain of and what she is uncertain of and whether the information she has is based on evidence or unverifiable beliefs and assumptions.

Placing the information from the scenario in the matrix and then reviewing its contents, Fiona not only has a quick synopsis of what happened, but she can easily see what she still needs to know. As soon as possible, Fiona will need

TABLE 1.2   *Fiona's Certainty Matrix (Pulling the Plug)*

	Certainties	**Uncertainties**
Warranted	*I know...* – Rick was removed from the school pending a meeting with Faculty of Education Professional Standards Committee.	*I don't know...* – the impact of Rick's behaviour on the victims and their families. – what will happen if the teacher candidates are unable to complete their scheduled practicums at Freemont High School.
Unwarranted	*I think I know...* – why Sheila blames the Faculty. – why Sheila expects Stan and I to agree to her demands. – what Rick's intentions were. – what is best for all.	*I ought to know...* – if this is a matter for the police. – why Sheila refuses to consult with others about the issue.

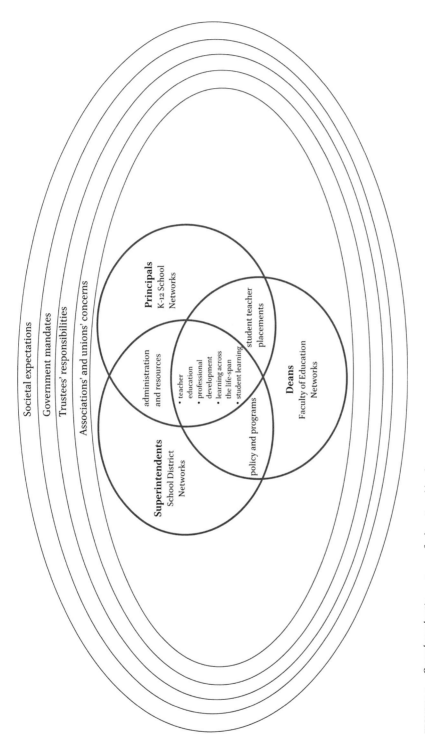

FIGURE 1.2   *Complex adaptive systems of educational leaders*

to find out how she can best help Rick's victims and their families access legal advice, and determine the fate of the rest of the cohort of teacher candidates at the school. Fiona determines that Sheila is basing her actions on assumptions and taken-for-granted beliefs. As her supervisor, Fiona needs to consider what guidance she can offer Sheila, especially in relation to her lack of understanding of the principal's position in the complex adaptive system in which Freemont High School operates.

Figure 1.2 is a representation of the kind of complex adaptive system in which educational institutions operate. It does not attempt to depict all of the constituents, such as students, parents, and staff, but rather focuses on superintendents, principals, and deans and their jurisdictions and overlapping responsibilities. It is assumed that members of senior leadership teams, associates, consultants, department heads, and directors of operations are subject to the same diverse pressures.

In the next chapter, we explore how educational leaders can understand uncertainty more deeply, particularly the challenges they inevitably face in complex adaptive systems. This leads us to consider how complexity leadership and *social capital* theories can help educational leaders navigate uncertainty.

References

Anastasion, D. (2016, November 1). The price of certainty. *The New York Times*. Retrieved from https://www.nytimes.com/2016/11/01/opinion/the-price-of-certainty.html

Ansell, C., & Boin, A. (2017). Taming deep uncertainty: The potential of pragmatist principles for understanding and improving strategic crisis management. *Administration & Society*, 1–34. doi:10.1177/0095399717747655

Bennett, N., & Lemoine, G. J. (2014). What VUCA really means for you. *Harvard Business Review, 92*(1–2), 27.

Blandin, N. M. (2008). *Re-conceptualizing leadership for an era of complexity and uncertainty: A case study of leadership in a complex adaptive system* (Ed.D. Thesis). The George Washington University, Washington, DC.

Davis, B., & Sumara, D. (2005). Complexity science and educational action research: Toward a pragmatics of transformation. *Educational Action Research, 13*(3), 453–466.

Descartes, R. (1701/1954). *Philosophical writings* (E. Anscombe & P. T. Geach, Trans.). Edinburgh: Nelson.

Dewey, J. (1933). *How we think: A restatement of the relation of reflective thinking to the educative process*. Boston, MA: D. C. Heath.

Duignan, P. A. (2003). *Formation of capable, influential and authentic leaders for times of uncertainty*. Paper presented at the Australian Primary Principals Association National Conference, Adelaide, Australia.

Floden, R. E., & Buchmann, M. (1993). Between routines and anarchy: Preparing teachers for uncertainty. *Oxford Review of Education, 19*(3), 373–382.

Floden, R. E., & Clark, C. M. (1988). Preparing teachers for uncertainty. *Teachers College Record, 89*(4), 505–524.

Fullan, M. (2008). *The six secrets of change: What the best leaders do to help their organizations survive and thrive*. San Francisco, CA: Jossey-Bass.

Goldstein, J. (1999). Emergence as a construct: History and issues. *Emergence, 1*(1), 49–72.

Grint, K. (2005). Problems, problems, problems: The social construction of leadership. *Human Relations, 58*(11), 1467–1494.

Handy, C. (1994). *The age of paradox*. Boston, MA: Harvard Business School Press.

Hasinoff, S., & Mandzuk, D. (2015). *Case studies in educational foundations: Canadian perspectives*. Don Mills: Oxford University Press.

Kahneman, D. (2011). *Thinking, fast and slow*. New York, NY: Farar, Straus, and Giroux.

Kelly, K. (1998). *New rules for the new economy: Ten radical strategies for a connected world*. New York, NY: Penguin Books.

Konnikova, M. (2013, April 30). Why we need answers. *The New Yorker*. Retrieved from https://www.newyorker.com/tech/elements/why-we-need-answers

Kosenko, K. (2014). Uncertainty management theory. In T. L. Thompson (Ed.), *Encyclopedia of health communication* (Vol. 3, pp. 1426–1427). Thousand Oaks, CA: Sage Publications Ltd.

Kruglanski, A. W., & Webster, D. M. (1996). Motivated closing of the mind: "Seizing" and "freezing." *Psychological Review, 103*(2), 263–283.

Lortie, D. C. (1975). *School teacher: A sociological study*. Chicago, IL: University of Chicago Press.

Mitleton-Kelly, E. (Ed.). (2003). *The principles of complexity and enabling infrastructures*. Oxford: Elsevier Science Ltd.

Montuori, A. (2013). Complexity and transdisciplinarity: Reflections on theory and practice. *World Futures, 69*(4–6), 200–230.

Morrison, K. (2010). Complexity theory, school leadership and management: Questions for theory and practice. *Educational Management Administration and Leadership, 38*(4), 374–393.

Pascale, R. T., Milleman, M., & Gioja, L. (2000). *Surfing the edge of chaos: The laws of nature and the new laws of business*. New York, NY: Crown Business.

Pelc, S. (2017). Marginality and Marginalization. In R. Chand, E. Nel, & S. Pelc (Eds.), *Societies, social inequalities and marginalization: Marginal regions in the 21st century* (pp. 13–28). Cham: Springer International Publishing.

Senge, P. (1995). *CEO thought summit/Interviewer: W. Kiechel.* MIT Sloan Management Review.

Shaked, H., & Schechter, C. (2017). *Systems thinking for school leaders: Holistic leadership for excellence in education.* Cham: Springer International Publishing.

Smith, W. K., Lewis, M. W., & Tushman, M. L. (2016). "Both/and" leadership. *Harvard Business Review, 94*(5), 62–70.

Sutherland, I. E. (2017). Learning and growing: Trust, leadership, and response to crisis. *Journal of Educational Administration, 55*(1), 2–17.

Thompson, J. D. (2003). *Organizations in action: Social science bases of administrative theory.* New York, NY: McGraw-Hill.

CHAPTER 2

Understanding Uncertainty

Understanding uncertainty in educational institutions requires an ability to distinguish between *basic problems* and *complex problems* or *dilemmas.* Whereas basic problems can be resolved relatively easily once a number of possible resolutions are identified, complex problems or dilemmas are messy (Lampert, 1985; Schon, 1987) and create a "disorienting experience in which our beliefs and sense making structures are severely hampered" (Ulmer, Sellnow, & Seeger, 2013, p. 102). Dilemmas "must first be recognized and then "unpacked" and pulled apart, in order to, at best, be managed" (Duignan & Collins, 2003, p. 283). The scenarios in this book are best described as complex problems or more specifically, *moral or social dilemmas,* rather than basic problems.

Dilemmas are symptomatic of life in complex adaptive systems. Therefore, it is not surprising that educational leaders must regularly confront dilemmas in their practice. According to Kidder (2005), the most difficult of these, "don't centre upon right versus wrong. They involve right versus right. They are genuine dilemmas precisely because each side is firmly rooted in core values" (p. 18). Soltis (1987) describes perplexing situations of this type as *moral dilemmas* because they are characterized by (1) our concern for the obligations we have to one another and what is the right thing to do, (2) the insufficiency of facts alone to effect resolution, and (3) the importance of understanding the principles that underlie our moral decisions.

Cook and State (2017) and others, focus their attention on "ubiquitous and intractable" social dilemmas which occur when "individual interests conflict with the collective interests of those involved" (p. 9). Social dilemmas provoke individuals to choose their own benefit over the good of society, despite knowing that the long-term interests of all are likely to be jeopardized. Van Lange et al. (2017) argue that social dilemmas "bring to the forefront motives such as selfishness, egalitarianism, and retaliation and emotions such as empathy, guilt, and shame" (p. vii). An example of a social dilemma in education occurs when teachers, who are long past the usual retirement age, continue to teach in spite of complaints about their performance and in staying on, stop younger, better prepared teachers from entering the workforce and prevent students from benefiting from new ideas.

In addition to moral and social dilemmas, educational leaders are less frequently faced with *crises* which may be intentional (i.e., terrorism, sabotage, or unethical leadership) or unintentional (i.e., natural disasters, disease outbreaks,

© KONINKLIJKE BRILL NV, LEIDEN, 2018 | DOI 10.1163/9789004368484_002

or product failures). Although crises are typically more urgent than dilemmas, the attributes identified by Mason et al. (2017) are arguably the same,

- they are often unexpected;
- they are non-routine and require novel and often extreme response
  measures;
- they produce high-levels of uncertainty;
- they create opportunities for learning, growth, and renewal; and,
- they may produce threats to image, reputation or high priority goals.
  (p. 232)

Given the prevalence of problems, dilemmas, and crises that educational
leaders face, it is no wonder that there are high turnover rates in educational
institutions or what Finnigan and Daly (2017) aptly call *leadership churn*.
They make the case that frequent changes of leadership can be a source
of uncertainty that "can potentially have a cascading disruptive impact,
from the superintendent's office all the way to the classroom" (p. 25). Apart
from causing disequilibrium in an educational system, a revolving door of
educational leaders stymies meaningful change and innovation. After all,
faculty and staff are unlikely to take new initiatives and priorities seriously
when they sense that reforms are temporary and likely to change with the next
administrator.

The difficulty in attracting and retaining suitable candidates and experienced
educational leaders for schools (Copland, 2001; Tingley, 1996) has been widely
reported. Furthermore, as Gmelch et al. (1999) suggest, finding and keeping
deans for faculties of education is no less of a problem. Less reported is that the
pool of applicants has always been unfairly limited by a kind of "tunnel vision
that sees only white males as viable candidates" (Tingley, 1996, p. 38).

In addition to the barriers erected by inherently biased hiring practices,
a number of important factors deter "the best and the brightest" from ever
seeking educational leadership positions, including the nature of the work
itself. Leadership positions are less attractive to those who want to work
directly with students or pursue academic research. For those who are attracted
by the work, they may be discouraged by "limited compensation, inadequate
preparation options, high stress, and lack of respect" (Copland, 2001, p. 530).
Exacerbating shortages that result from difficulties in recruitment are the
difficulties jurisdictions experience in retaining existing administrators.
Currently, there are a greater than normal number of retirees as a result of
demographic variables, but there is also an increasing number who are leaving
leadership positions due to "shifting educational demands, huge workloads,

and lack of job security" (Copland, 2001, p. 529). According, to Copland (2001), the burgeoning expectations of the educational leadership role is perhaps the greatest deterrent to those considering a career in administration or remaining in it. For example, those thinking about becoming educational leaders are now expected to be,

– instructional leaders for increasingly diverse student populations;
– skilled negotiators with boards and labor unions;
– insightful counselors who solve personal and professional problems;
– efficient managers of finance and physical plants;
– successful fundraisers;
– architects of positive institutional climates;
– welcoming advocates to community members;
– highly capable stewards of professional development;
– data analysts who make careful evidence-based decisions; and,
– innovative visionaries who guide their institutions effectively through difficult times.

We may well have reached a "tipping point" (Gladwell, 2000) in which the expectations of educational leaders far exceed what any single person can deliver. Furthermore, those who accept leadership positions find that they must do so with diminishing resources and support, greater pressure to deliver academic excellence, and increasingly complex technologies. However, as we indicated in the previous chapter, perhaps the greatest challenge for educational leaders is the inherent uncertainty embedded in educational systems. Indeed, Thompson (1967) suggests that uncertainty "appears as the fundamental problem for complex organizations and coping with uncertainty as the essence of the administrative process" (p. 159).

As Clarke (2013) points out, the "uncertainty, ambiguity, interdependencies and interrelatedness that now characterize the environments in which organizations operate has shifted our understanding of leadership away from its traditional individualistic focus to a more collective, social concept" (p. 135). For an explanation of what this shift means for educational leaders, we turn to complexity leadership theory for direction.

1   Complexity Leadership Theory

Although Complexity Leadership Theory draws deeply from complex adaptive systems theory, it nevertheless recognizes that emergence and self-organiza-

tion in biological or ecological systems look quite different in social institutions (Uhl-Bien, Marion, & McKelvey, 2007). Indeed, Morrison (2010) argues
that,

> ...self-organization and emergent order may be unsafe in some
> situations, and control may be necessary, for example, in the military or
> prisons in high reliability organizations or in 'total institutions' such as
> schools, psychiatric hospitals and orphanages. (p. 382)

Complexity Leadership Theory, therefore, envisions three functions of
leadership, namely, *administrative, adaptive,* and *enabling leadership.*
Administrative leadership is a formal function that is essential for "apply[ing]
proven solutions to known problems" and for coordinating and structuring
organizational activities (Uhl-Bien et al., 2007, p. 300). To do so, educational
leaders are often obliged to use "tightening" behaviors to reduce "variance
through choice, execution, standardization, and restricting information
flows" (Uhl-Bien, 2012). In other words, it is through this formal, hierarchical,
bureaucratic, and managerial function that educational leaders establish and
maintain the norms necessary for the smooth operation of an educational
system.

Adaptive leadership comes into play when educational leaders are
confronted with "adaptive challenges" or what we have previously referred to
as dilemmas. Uhl-Bien et al. (2007) argue that adaptive leadership is necessary
when "groups need to learn their way out of problems that could not have
been predicted" (p. 300). Under such circumstances, educational leaders need
to encourage emergent activities through "loosening" behaviors that enable
"interaction, search, experimentation and information flows" in their social
networks (Uhl-Bien, 2012).

Enabling leadership operates at the interface of administrative and adaptive
leadership by generating the conditions necessary for creative problem-
solving, adaptability, and learning and by facilitating the flow of information.
Perhaps the most important condition necessary is the trust that is generated
and sustained in a network through enabling leadership rather than people's
knowledge and skills, also known as their human capital. As Clarke (2013)
points out,

> Leadership is the property of relationships, no longer residing in one
> individual. Instead of human capital, the focus in leadership development
> shifts towards the development of social capital. (p. 136)

Below we delve more deeply into social capital, particularly the norms established through administrative leadership, the networks sustained through adaptive leadership, and the trust that is necessary for enabling leadership.

2   Social Capital

Putnam (1993), whose definition of social capital is widely cited, suggests that it refers to the "features of social organizations, such as trust, norms, and networks that can improve the efficiency of society by facilitating coordinated actions" (p. 67). In the remainder of this chapter, we look more closely at norms, networks, and trust and then discuss a scenario that illustrates how understanding each of these three sources of social capital can be helpful for educational leaders.

Considering that "accomplishing work through others is the essence of leadership" (Brass & Krackhardt, 1999, p. 180) and that educational institutions can be understood as "systems of relationships" (Kershner & McQuillan, 2016, p. 9), it is not surprising that social capital has become central to the conceptualization of educational leadership. Social capital is acknowledged to be a generally positive and valuable resource for leaders (Brass & Krackhardt, 1999; Kershner & McQuillan, 2016; King, 2004), but in times of uncertainty, when complex problems or intractable dilemmas can push educational systems to the edge of chaos, it is thought to be critical. As Brass and Krackhardt (1999) point out, "Social capital becomes more important as environments become more volatile and the boundaries of decision-making become more permeable" (p. 191).

Although social capital has been notoriously difficult to pin down, the basic premise is that "one's family, friends, and associates constitute an important asset, one that can be called upon in a crisis, enjoyed for its own sake, and/or leveraged for material gain" (Woolcock, 2001, p. 12). Some of the attributes of social capital that King (2004) lists help us to understand why this is this case,

> The literature describes social capital as an appropriable resource, a resource that can be exchanged or combined. Social capital can appreciate over time with use and investment but will depreciate with non-use or abuse. It can complement other resources. As a resource, stocks of social capital are often reinforcing and cumulative. (p. 474)

Simply put, relationships have value (Burt, 2000).

Woolcock (2001) cautions, however, that "social capital cannot be understood independently of its broader institutional environment" (p. 13) or what Bourdieu (1986) referred to as the *social field*. In complexity leadership terms, the environmental context is referred to as the *adaptive space* where the conditions may or may not be conducive for the development of social capital (Arena & Uhl-Bien, 2016, p. 25). Clearly, not all social arrangements are sources of social capital and not all educational leaders take advantage of the social capital that accrues in their environment. Both institutional and personal factors can be expected to affect the degree to which educational leaders are able to develop and access social capital. Once educational leaders understand and mobilize social capital through the establishment of norms, the cultivation of networks, and the development of trust, the effectiveness of their educational institution and its chances for survival can be expected to improve (Tsang, 2010).

3   Norms

When a norm exists and is effective, it constitutes a powerful, though sometimes fragile, form of social capital. Effective norms that inhibit crime make it possible to walk freely outside at night in a city and enable us to leave our houses without fear for our safety. Norms in a community that support and provide effective rewards for high achievement in school greatly facilitate a school's task (Coleman, 1988, p. S104). According to Fukuyama (2001) the norms that constitute social capital can range from a *norm of reciprocity* between two friends which governs the exchange of favors up to complex and elaborately articulated doctrines like Christianity or Confucianism. As he points out,

> Not just any set of instantiated norms constitutes social capital; they must lead to cooperation in groups and therefore are related to traditional virtues like honesty, the keeping of commitments, reliable performance of duties, reciprocity, and the like. (Fukuyama, 2001, p. 3)

Most norms are understood implicitly and followed quietly without much controversy, but increasingly, educational leaders are finding it beneficial to articulate what is acceptable behavior for faculty, staff, parents, and students and to delineate sanctions if norms are violated. Norms now appear on wall posters, are incorporated into mission statements, and fill the pages of handbooks written to ensure the smooth running of our educational institutions. Norms, such as these, are also embedded in the *hidden curriculum* of educational institutions. These shape behaviour and foster a positive institutional culture through the maintenance of institutional traditions, nonverbal cues, and overt rewards and punishments. It is interesting to note in this regard that school uniforms, once the hallmark of private schools, are increasingly being adopted in public schools in order to make expectations about dress unambiguous and transparent.

One benefit of broadly shared norms is that network members do not have to constantly negotiate a set of rules to ensure the smooth operation of the institution. Network members who agree on the *norms of collaboration* for example, benefit from running punctual meetings in which every voice is heard, and conversations remain focused on agenda items (Garmston & Wellman, 2016). Furthermore, as Fukuyama (2001) reminds us, "No contract can possibly specify every contingency that may arise between the parties; most presuppose a certain amount of goodwill that prevents the parties from taking advantage of unforeseen loopholes" (p. 10). Therefore, agreed upon norms can "substitute for the formal contracts, incentives, and monitoring mechanisms that are otherwise necessary" (Fu, 2004, p. 24). Kahne et al. (2001) summarize the way norms create social capital in educational institutions this way,

> Norms can provide powerful incentives for particular behaviors (e.g., emphasizing literacy-based or direct instruction or a particular style of interaction with the community), priorities (e.g., success on specific tests or attention to specific issues such as multiculturalism or literacy), and attitudes (e.g., commitment to excellence or hard work). Norms can create forms of coherence that facilitate attractive partnerships. They can also provide a sense of direction and criteria for accountability. (p. 436)

Norms that constitute a source of social capital can also have a downside. While compliance with norms maintains order and engenders a sense of security for members of social networks, it can come at a cost. The close monitoring and excessive pressures to conform can stifle creativity and restrict our ability to respond adaptively to uncertainty. Moreover, dense, tight groups, such as cliques, gangs, or even exclusive dyadic relationships, can develop idiosyncratic norms that set them so far apart from their broader social networks that they become alienated from institutional goals.

A less extreme example of what happens when the norms of one group differ from those of other groups plays out in many staffrooms. The sharing of research and new ideas can be effectively marginalized when anti-intellectual staff members claim that those who value intellectual conversations are "interrupting their break." The need to decompress in staffrooms is certainly understandable. However, continual rejection of deeper discussions may stem from an unwillingness to entertain any new ideas that run contrary to the unexamined norms that underpin much of our knowledge as educators. As we point out in an earlier work (Hasinoff & Mandzuk, 2015), it is no easy process to overcome our unwarranted certainties and "since we tend to look for confirmation rather than refutation of what we already know, our assumptions, theories, and taken-for-granted beliefs can become significant barriers to critical thinking" (Hasinoff & Mandzuk, 2015, p. xxi). We need to actively resist our natural desire for certainty and predictability by consciously disrupting prevailing norms and ensuring that we have solid evidence for what we do.

Since norms are transmitted, monitored, and reinforced in social networks, the two can sometimes be difficult to disentangle. In the next section we consider networks separately with the understanding that they do not actually exist apart from norms. Networks are a source of social capital for adaptive leaders who creatively develop emergent leadership and self-organization to meet the changing needs of their respective educational institutions.

4   Networks

Although most of us would describe the relationships in our professional social networks as generally positive and some as being particularly close, this is not always or necessarily the case. Relationships, even the closest ones, may flounder at times and when they do, our ability to function effectively as educational leaders may become strained and difficult. In fact, it is important to note that relationships in social networks are fluid and that,

> Leadership will require identifying and nurturing potential relationships, putting the right people together in the right place at the right time, only to realize that this combination of people, places, and times will soon change. (Brass & Krackhardt, 1999, p. 180)

Faced with the uncertainties inherent in relationships, educational leaders can benefit from an increased understanding of the nature of social networks and how social capital is developed within and between them.

In a nutshell, social networks are a set of related *nodes* and *ties*. The nodes can refer either to individuals or groups or even institutions and the ties refer to the connections between them. Granovetter (1973) describes network connections as "weak" or "strong" ties, depending on the strength of the association between them. Ties formed through friendship, are examples of strong ties, involving a great deal of time, emotional intensity, intimacy, and reciprocity whereas ties formed between acquaintances are described as weak since they involve little time, are generally superficial, and may even be one directional. Granovetter (1973) helps us recognize the strength of weak ties that enable us to "bridge" to individuals or groups to whom we might not otherwise have access and thereby gain valuable new insights and resources. While acknowledging the value of Granovetter's argument about the importance of weak ties, Krackhardt (1992) reminds us of the strength of strong ties. After all, it is strong ties that help to overcome people's natural resistance to change and mitigate their discomfort with uncertainty, especially in times of insecurity or crisis.

The notion of weak and strong ties is embedded in the two distinct, but not mutually exclusive, dimensions of social capital identified by Putnam (2000) as *bonding* and *bridging* social capital. Bonding is generated in close inward-looking relations between like-minded individuals with strong ties, such as family members, close friends, and neighbors (Woolcock, 2001, p. 13). Bridging, on the other hand, develops in more outward-looking relations between people with weak ties who have different interests and goals, such as acquaintances, associates, and colleagues. In capturing the distinction between these two dimensions, Putnam (2000) suggests that "bonding social capital constitutes a kind of sociological superglue whereas bridging social capital provides a sociological WD-40" (p. 23).

5   Bonding

Bonding social capital accrues in dense, close networks where the norms of reciprocity, obligations, and expectations create reserves of trust. These kinds of cohesive networks are characterized by increased communication and information flow, greater coordination of resources to achieve common goals, and lower transaction costs. The result is that networks high in bonding social capital are better able to preserve or maintain their resources (Lin, 1999). For example, Putnam (2004) points out the educational resources students can derive from their peer networks,

> Inside the walls, it is widely recognized, peer networks *among students* have a powerful effect both on aspiration levels and on the educational

process itself. This phenomenon is even more marked, in the US at least, at the university level, where some evidence suggests that college students learn more from one another than they do from formal instruction. (p. 4)

Bonding social capital becomes especially important for educational leaders in times of difficulty. For one thing, when complex problems or even crises arise, members of closed networks are easily available and greatly motivated to help one another (Granovetter, 1973; Krackhardt, 1992; Moran, 2005). When faced with disequilibrium in the environment, educational leaders can obtain psychological, social, and even financial support from the members of their social networks and enlist them to take whatever collective actions are necessary to buffer the institution in a crisis and protect its core mission (Ryu, 2017, p. 407).

The downside of bonding, however, is that the very properties (e.g., closure, stability, interdependence, and shared ideologies) that allow those with strong ties to derive great benefit from social capital means inevitably that some other people will be marginalized, silenced, or even excluded from social networks in which they have a right to belong. Such disparities can become exacerbated and embedded in social structures as Kwon and Adler (2014) point out,

> The inequalities characterizing contemporary social relations – of wealth and income, between races and genders – shape social capital very deeply, and in turn, social capital is implicated in both the reproduction of these inequalities and in movements attempting to challenge them. (p. 7)

At their most extreme, tight, closed, insulated networks can function like gangs, whose leaders wield social capital as a club to abuse power, ignore conflicts of interest, and reduce personal autonomy. Such leaders may actively work against the efforts of network members to adopt new and different ideas or access resources from outside the group. As a consequence, some networks that are tightly bonded have few and largely redundant sources of information. Like the messages in the children's game of "Postman," information can became easily distorted as it cycles and recycles through the network. Avoiding input from outside networks can lead to narrow decisions that fail to address rapid changes in the environment. Such behaviors often represent a misguided attempt to preserve the status quo or equilibrium of the system. However, the costs may be too high, when there is undue pressure on members to "toe the line," when congeniality is contrived (Hargreaves, 1991), creativity is reduced, and group-think (Janis, 1982) becomes pervasive.

Communication is very closely linked to trust. Levels of trust seem to increase not only with clearer communication, but also when there is more of it. (Principal)

6   Bridging

Bridging social capital accrues in relationships based on structurally less dense and fragile weak ties (Krackhardt, 1992). As individuals with weak ties bridge to others in different networks, they are able to expand their reach and access new and different information and resources. Burt (2000) refers to the spaces to be bridged in social structures as *structural holes*. He argues that these are a source of social capital because they offer "an opportunity to broker the flow of information between people, and control the projects that bring together people from opposite sides of the hole" (p. 353). In other words, educational leaders can act as *boundary spanners* to access different resources than those already available in their own networks and thereby enhance the performance of their institutions (Ryu, 2017). For example, educational leaders who solicit donations from businesses, attract volunteers, arrange for student mentors, or make sure that their governing councils are widely representative of the groups they serve are using bridging social capital to enhance the effectiveness of their institutions.

In times of difficulty, educational leaders who are able to bridge to other networks may also be able to buffer the effects of changes in their own institution by learning from others who have had similar experiences. Furthermore, Marshall and Stolle (2004) argue that "positive experiences with dissimilar individuals will have greater effects on the development of generalized trust than will relations with individuals who are similar to oneself in terms of characteristics, attitudes and behaviors" (p. 129).

Like bonding social capital, bridging social capital has some limitations and downsides. For example, educational leaders who spend too much time out of their institutions pursuing bridging social capital may lose sight of internal priorities and compromise their internal network relationships. In times of difficulty, the resources needed to overcome environmental uncertainties are unlikely to come from individuals in other organizations that are themselves experiencing scarcity. As Ryu (2017) points out,

> Members tied weakly share a relatively low level of trust, and they cannot guarantee the rule of reciprocity when everyone is suffering. In such a situation, it is likely that members with bridging social capital find it difficult to help one another. (p. 407)

When comparing bonding and bridging social capital, Putnam (2000) makes a relevant distinction between "getting by" and "getting ahead." Bonding social capital involves trust and reciprocity in closed networks and helps the process of getting by in life on a daily basis. Getting ahead, in contrast, is facilitated through the crosscutting ties that take the form of bridging social capital (Coffé & Geys, 2007, p. 124). Putnam (2000) argues that we need to both "get by" and "get ahead" so that to bond or bridge is not an "either-or" proposition; rather, it is a matter of "more or less" (p. 23). Indeed, stressing one or the other may lead to better performance in the short term but different and not necessarily positive outcomes in the long term.

Ryu (2017) argues that,

> [T]oo much attention to one aspect of social capital in a time of peace can lead to failure of an organization in a time of difficulty...strategic choices between bonding and bridging social capital are contingent on the level of environmental uncertainty. (p. 415)

At times of uncertainty, educational leaders may do best to look to bonding social capital "from those whose qualities, skills, and know-how are complementary to their own and relevant to solving the problem at hand" (Kwon & Adler, 2014, p. 5). Similarly, educational leaders need to understand the importance of balancing bonding and bridging social capital when implementing reforms and adopting innovations within their institutions. Achieving such a balance is critical for developing institutional cultures in which leadership can emerge from all levels of the system yet all members of the network are bound together by a shared ideology to accomplish common goals. Indeed, Kilduff and Balkundi (2011) suggest,

> Leadership can be understood as social capital that collects around certain individuals – whether formally designated as leaders or not – based on the acuity of their social perceptions and the structure of social ties. (p. 120)

The clear implication for both current and emergent educational leaders is that social capital is most likely to accrue to those who are able to interact well with others, have accurate perceptions of themselves and others, and are skilled in communication. As Balkundi and Kilduff (2006) state,

> If a leader wants to use social network ties to lead others, the leader must be able to perceive the existence, nature, and structure of these ties – not

just the ties surrounding the leader, but the ties connecting others in the
organization both near and far. (p. 424)

In the next section we focus the discussion on *trust* with the understanding
that, as a source of social capital, it is highly entangled with norms and
networks and does not exist apart from either (Nickerson, 2009, p. 186).
Enabling leadership, which operates at the interface of administrative and
adaptive leadership, generates the conditions of trust that are critical for the
maintenance and survival of educational institutions.

7   Trust

In addition to a vast literature on the subject, there is increasing attention on
the role and importance of trust in healthy educational institutions (Bligh, 2016;
Bryk & Schneider, 2003; Finnigan & Daly, 2017; Sutherland, 2017; Tschannen-
Moran, 2014; Tschannen-Moran & Hoy, 1998). Trust is so closely identified with
social capital that the two concepts are often used interchangeably. In this
section, we clarify the relationship between trust and social capital and show
how understanding trust in relationships can help educational leaders make
sense of the complex problems in their educational settings.

To begin with, there is no getting away from the fact that trust is an elusive
and contested concept. For example, some researchers consider trust to be a
necessary precondition for social capital (Woolcock, 2001) whereas others
argue that trust is a consequence of social capital (Flores & Solomon, 1998). We
agree with those like Fu (2004) who characterize trust as both a precursor and
a result of social capital. After all, without first developing trust in relationships,
educational leaders cannot expect to be able to access and mobilize social
capital and when they access social capital, they can expect to extend and
deepen trust within and between their networks. Simply put, "[I]ndividuals can
interact more effectively with high levels of trust" (Finnigan & Daly, 2017, p. 24).

Trust in relationships can create many benefits for an educational
institution, notably that it,

> ...can strengthen norms of reciprocity, diminish the amount of energy
> lost to suspicion, unresolved issues, and associated uncertainty anxiety
> that otherwise often results in blame, gossip, resentment, and frustration.
> It also reduces the time spent in the slow, expensive process of defining,
> monitoring, and guaranteeing compliance – the detailed process of
> enforcement. (Fu, 2004, p. 24)

In hierarchical contexts, such as educational institutions, we cannot ignore the differences of power and status in the development of trust (Bourdieu & Coleman, 1991). Although trusting relationships in the workplace are often reciprocal, they are never symmetrical. Indeed, differences in authority mean supervisors and their employees have different perspectives about trust that can create conflicting expectations (Bligh, 2016). For example, supervisors "report that being open to ideas, availability, and discreteness are the most important aspects of trustworthy followers" whereas followers report that "availability, competence, discreteness, integrity, and openness are more important for trust in the leader" (Bligh, 2016, p. 31).

No matter how trusting we may be, we simply cannot and do not trust everyone equally. Of course, we need to have what Solomon and Flores (2001) refer to as a *basic trust* that others will generally do what we expect them to do in order to function as a society. Otherwise, it would not be safe to travel alone or depend, for example, on the values of our currency in a simple transaction.

I want everyone to have a basic level of trust in me. I want my colleagues and subordinates to realize that I have a positive intent and that whatever actions I take are done to help, support, teach, and lead rather than to be intentionally negative or harmful. (Superintendent)

Beyond basic trust, most of us are fortunate enough to be able to trust a few people profoundly and to take unreserved comfort in these relationships. Such *profound trust* or what Solomon and Flores (2001) refer to as authentic trust "takes into account the capabilities and history of the person being trusted, recognizes a risk, and makes the conscious choice to trust anyway" (p. 31). Profound trust is highly prized, but relatively rare. It is most likely to be found in bonding relationships which exhibit the properties of closure, stability, interdependence, and shared ideology.

I share profound trust with those who bring forward the fewest issues. They trust my decision-making and they trust what's happening overall. They believe that I am acting in their best interest and on their behalf. (Dean)

Since profound trust involves the emotional connections that bind people together, it is not surprising that people feel most betrayed when this type of trust is broken. Indeed, many of us have discovered too late that what we thought was profound trust was premature or even blind trust. When it turns out that our profound trust is unmerited or unreciprocated, we are upset not only because of the other person's betrayal, but also because we feel foolish for having extended our trust recklessly in the first place. Trust always involves risk, however, since, we cannot know for certain that our profound trust is warranted or reciprocated until it is tested.

The fact is that we don't know most people well enough to trust them profoundly. In some cases we may even have reasons to believe that we cannot or should not trust certain people. For these reasons, the trust we extend to most others can be thought of as *provisional trust.* That is, we may be willing to trust people up to a certain point or under certain circumstances, but not at other times or in other circumstances. Provisional trust is characteristic of the relationships we have with acquaintances, most of our colleagues, those with whom we are not familiar, or those with whom we have weak ties.

Whether our trust in relationships is provisional or profound, it is based as Bligh (2016) points out, on "an expectation or belief that one can rely on another person's actions *and* words and that the person has good intentions to carry out their promises" (p. 22). When expectations are not met or promises turn out to be empty, trust is broken. Trust can be extremely fragile and as Tschannen-Moran and Hoy (1998) caution, "the nature of a trusting relationship can be altered instantaneously with a simple comment, a betrayed confidence, or a decision that violates the sense of care one has expected of another" (p. 335). One of the superintendents we interviewed quoted a familiar maxim that underscores this fragility, "Trust takes years to build, seconds to break, and forever to repair."

Whether a breakdown in trust is caused by one person, who intentionally or unintentionally violates trust, or is the consequence of ill-advised systemic changes, the effect can be highly destructive to an educational institution. As Duncan (2015) suggests, "when trust is damaged, faculty members may tend to seek safety, to work in isolation, and to concentrate on areas that are beneficial to their own career path rather than the collective progress of the unit as a whole" (p. 32). Furthermore, changes to personnel, whether as a result of the leadership churn we discussed earlier or as a result of movement of personnel within the institution, can alter the trust relationships in the networks that make up a system. Finnigan and Daly (2017) explain that,

> ...when someone who is a trusted colleague, key listener, helpful resource, friend, or confidant leaves a school, that departure creates a hole that's hard to fill. The departure can involve a loss of knowledge, social support, and institutional memory. Moreover, it can create a sense of instability and disrupt routines, which in turn can lead to a loss of productivity. (p. 25)

Although we cannot always prevent difficult situations or crises from happening, we can adapt our behavior to minimize the damage when they do occur and focus our efforts on repairing broken trust. Nevertheless, Sutherland (2017) reminds us that, "During times of crisis it is too late to begin banking trust. The stores of trust must be there already, as a result of the way the school does business and the community functions" (p. 13). Bryk and Schneider (2003) explain why this is so important in educational systems,

> When school professionals trust one another and sense support from parents, they feel safe to experiment with new practices. Similarly, relational trust fosters the necessary social exchanges among school professionals as they learn from one another. Talking honestly with colleagues about what's working and what's not means exposing your own ignorance and making yourself vulnerable. Without trust, genuine conversations of this sort remain unlikely.

As the incoming dean in the following scenario discovers, trust makes all the difference when educational leaders take on a project that requires "all hands on deck."

8   Puppet on a String

Sophia Grant-Farquar was delighted to be the new Dean of the Faculty of Education in a small, research-intensive university on the east coast. Her appointment was well received because she was a well-qualified and trusted colleague and would bring her experience as an Indigenous elder to the position. However, not everyone was happy about her long-standing relationship with her mentor, Blair Vitelli, the outgoing Dean.

Sophia had been Blair's graduate student for both her M.Ed. and her Ph.D. degrees and it was widely believed that he had an undue influence on her decisions, even after she graduated. Like some other members of the faculty, Sophia was enthralled with Blair, a nationally recognized scholar in Comparative Education and two-time national grant winner. However, he was not held in high esteem by everyone on the faculty. Although his supporters regarded him as charismatic, quick thinking, and decisive, other faculty members saw him as arrogant, self-serving, and autocratic. In fact, a few years back, Allison Harper and Monte Caldwell had staged a small scale revolt to have him removed from office or, at the very least, not renewed for another term.

The university responded to the "rebellion" by ignoring it. When the Provost announced that he planned to support the renewal of Blair's appointment, some of Blair's most vocal opponents left, leaving Allison and Monte to head the group that still opposed him. Three of the "rebels" accepted offers at other universities and a fourth retired early. Although everyone knew why their colleagues had "jumped ship," Blair refused to acknowledge his role in the exodus and spoke about the opportunities the faculty now had for renewal. Albert Mankowitz, however, left no doubt among his colleagues why he was leaving when he announced that he "couldn't stay one more day in this toxic environment."

It was clear that neither Allison nor Monte was prepared to let anyone forget about Blair's tenure as dean. Kendra Noseworthy, Sophia's confidante and associate dean, overheard Allison tell two of the new hires that even though Blair was on sabbatical, he was still pulling Sophia's strings. In truth, it was beginning to look that way.

Just last week, he hijacked the faculty council meeting and Sophia, who, as usual, supported his position, had done nothing to stop him. By the end of the meeting, Blair had successfully pressured the faculty to host an international conference on comparative education the following summer. As a result, the faculty was more deeply divided than ever. Blair's supporters pointed to the reputational benefits to the faculty, but Sophia knew that this kind of project would require everyone to get on board and that was far from certain. Those opposed, like Monte, were unlikely to contribute much effort and that would put added strain on those who agreed to volunteer for this time-consuming project. After the meeting, Monte complained to Sophia that she had handed Blair a "bully pulpit" and accused her of being a "dean by proxy." Sophia wasn't sure that Monte's accusations were fair but she realized with gut-wrenching certainty that her task of building trust in this group was going to be an uphill battle. The question was, "How could she continue to support Blair without appearing to be his puppet?"

Sophia is unsure where to begin, but she feels certain that trust is an issue in the faculty and that she will need to carve out a place that is independent of the former dean and his priorities. She decides to put her thoughts down in a Certainty Matrix to sort out what she knows and how she knows it.

Looking at the Certainty Matrix, Sophia sees that she needs to determine just how much work hosting an international conference will entail for the faculty. It will be helpful for her to talk to past organizers of the conference

TABLE 2.1   *Sophia's Certainty Matrix (Puppet on a String)*

	Certainties	Uncertainties
Warranted	*I know that...* – Allison and Monte don't trust Blair or me – I can count on Kendra – I will need to prove that I am independent of Blair – everyone needs to be on board if the conference is going to be successful	*I don't know...* – how much my support for Blair has contributed to perceptions that I am a weak leader – whether the strain on faculty members will be worth the benefits of hosting the conference
Unwarranted	*I think I know...* – why faculty think that Blair still runs the show – why faculty are divided about hosting an international conference	*I ought to know...* – what hosting an international conference entails – what assistance is available from past organizers and the university to help with the conference – how to encourage everyone to contribute to the success of the conference

and to find out what resources she can tap into from the university. As far as the faculty is concerned, Sophia knows that a really successful conference should involve the whole faculty in one way or another. However, she knows that Alison and Monte do not trust Blair or her. In fact, she knows that they consider her to be Blair's proxy. Sophia is concerned that these two may succeed in persuading other faculty members not to help simply because the conference was Blair's idea.

Sophia is in the difficult position of having to choose between her obligations to the faculty and the expectations of her mentor. Moreover, as long as she allows Blair free rein to dominate faculty council meetings, the provisional trust that she had so carefully built up with the rest of her colleagues and the profound trust she has built up with Kendra is likely to dissipate. She realizes that she will need to get to work quickly to find out who she can count on and who is only mildly disaffected. In particular, she will need to determine how to engage Allison and Monte and any others who are opposed.

Sophia is beginning to realize that demonstrating her independence from Blair may be the key to creating and sustaining trust in the faculty. Her recent performance at the faculty meeting suggests that "old habits die hard" and she may need to seek coaching to handle the meetings with a more even hand. She might consider spending time at the next faculty meeting discussing norms of collaboration so that no single person, including Blair, can dominate the meeting or distract participants from sticking to the agenda.

In the next chapter, we will consider how sensemaking can help educational leaders like Sophia deal with complex problems and crises in their institutions. We introduce a 5-step approach that educational leaders can use to sort through what they know and how they know it, and to consider what they can do to repair their relationships when trust breaks down.

References

Anastasion, D. (2016, November 1). The price of certainty. *The New York Times*. Retrieved from https://www.nytimes.com/2016/11/01/opinion/the-price-of-certainty.html

Arena, M., & Uhl-Bien, M. (2016). Complexity leadership theory: Shifting from human capital to social capital. *People + Strategy, 39*(2), 22–27.

Balkundi, P., & Kilduff, M. (2006). The ties that lead: A social network approach to leadership. *The Leadership Quarterly, 17*, 416–439. doi: 10.1016/j.leaqua.2005.09.004

Bligh, M. C. (2016). Leadership and trust. In J. Marques & S. Dhiman (Eds.), *Leadership today* (pp. 21–42). Switzerland: Springer International.

Bourdieu, P. (1986). The forms of capital. In J. Richardson (Ed.), *Handbook of theory and research for the sociology of education* (pp. 241–258). New York, NY: Greenwood.

Bourdieu, P., & Coleman, J. S. (1991). *Social theory for a changing society*. New York, NY: Russell Sage Foundation.

Brass, D., & Krackhardt, D. (1999). The social capital of twenty-first century leaders. In J. G. Hunt, G. Dodge, & L. Wong (Eds.), *Out of the box leadership: Transforming the twenty-first century army and other top performing organizations* (pp. 179–194). Stamford, CT: JAI Press.

Bryk, A., & Schneider, B. (2003). Trust in schools: A core resource for school reform. *Educational Leadership, 60*(6), 40–45. Retrieved from http://www.ascd.org/publications/educational-leadership/mar03/vol60/num06/Trust-in-Schools@-A-Core-Resource-for-School-Reform.aspx

Burt, R. (2000). The network structure of social capital. *Organizational Behaviour, 22*, 345–423.

Clarke, N. (2013). Model of complexity leadership development. *Human Resource Development International, 16*(2), 135–150.

Coffé, H., & Geys, B. (2007). Toward an empirical characterization of bridging and bonding social capital. *Nonprofit and Voluntary Sector Quarterly, 36*(1), 121–139.

Coleman, J. S. (1988). Social capital in the creation of human capital. *American Journal of Sociology, 94*, s95–s120.

Cook, K. S., & State, B. (2017). Trust and social dilemmas: A selected review of evidence and applications. In P. A. M. Van Lange, B. Rockenbach, & T. Yamagishi (Eds.), *Trust in social dilemmas* (pp. 9–32). New York, NY: Oxford University Press.

Copland, M. A. (2001). The myth of superprincipal. *Phi Delta Kappan, 82*(7), 528–533.

Duignan, P. A., & Collins, V. (2003). Leadership challenges and tensions in service organisations. In M. C. Bennett & M. Cartwright (Eds.), *Leadership of effective education*. Milton Keynes: Open University Press.

Duncan, H. E. (2015). Exploring complexities of leadership for teacher education. In S. E. Elliot-Johns (Ed.), *Leadership for change in teacher education: Voices of Canadian deans of education*. Rotterdam, The Netherlands: Sense Publishers.

Finnigan, K. S., & Daly, A. J. (2017). The trust gap: Understanding the effect of leadership churn in school districts. *American Educator, 41*(2), 24–29, 43.

Flores, F., & Solomon, R. C. (1998). Creating trust. *Business Ethics Quarterly, 8*(2), 205–232.

Fu, Q. (2004). *Trust, social capital, and organizational effectiveness* (Master of Public and International Affairs). Virginia Polytechnic Institute and State University, Blacksburg, VA.

Fukuyama, F. (2001). Social capital and civil society. *Third World Quarterly, 22*(1), 7–20.

Garmston, R. J., & Wellman, B. M. (2016). *The adaptive school: A sourcebook for developing collaborative groups* (3rd ed.). Lanham, MD: Rowman & Littlefield.

Gladwell, M. (2000). *The tipping point: How little things can make a big difference*. Boston, MA: Little Brown.

Gmelch, W. H., Wolverton, M., Wolverton, M. L., & Sarros, J. C. (1999). The academic dean: An imperiled species searching for balance. *Research in Higher Education, 40*, 717–740.

Granovetter, M. (1973). The strength of weak ties. *American Journal of Sociology, 78*, 1360–1380.

Hargreaves, A. (1991). Contrived collegiality: The micropolitics of teacher collaboration. In J. Blase (Ed.), *The politics of life in schools: Power, conflict, and cooperation* (pp. 46–72). Newbury Park, CA: Corwin.

Hasinoff, S., & Mandzuk, D. (2015). *Case studies in educational foundations: Canadian perspectives*. Don Mills: Oxford University Press.

Janis, I. L. (1982). *Groupthink: Psychological studies of policy decisions and fiascoes*. Boston, MA: Houghton Mifflin.

Kahne, J., O'Brien, J., Brown, A., & Quinn, T. (2001). Leveraging social capital and school improvement: The case of a school network and a comprehensive community initiative in Chicago. *Educational Administration Quarterly, 37*, 429–461.

Kershner, B., & McQuillan, P. (2016). Complex adaptive schools: Educational leadership and school change. *Complicity: An International Journal of Complexity and Education, 13*(1), 4–29.

Kidder, R. (2005). *How good people make tough choices: Resolving the dilemmas of ethical living* (2nd ed.). New York, NY: Institute for Global Ethics.

Kilduff, M., & Balkundi, P. (2011). A network approach to leader cognition and effectiveness. In A. Bryman, D. Collinson, K. Grint, B. Jackson, & M. Uhl-Bien (Eds.), *The Sage handbook of leadership* (pp. 118–135). Los Angeles, CA: Sage Publications.

King, N. (2004). Social capital and nonprofit leaders. *Nonprofit Management and Leadership, 14*(4), 471–486.

Krackhardt, D. (1992). The strength of strong ties: The importance of Philos in organizations. In N. Nohria & R. Eccles (Eds.), *Networks and organizations: Structure, form, and action* (pp. 216–239). Boston, MA: Harvard Business School Press.

Kwon, S.-W., & Adler, P. S. (2014). Social capital: Maturation of a field of research. *Academy of Management Review, 39*(4), 412–422.

Lampert, M. (1985). How do teachers manage to teach? Perspectives on problems of practice. *Harvard Educational Review, 55*(2), 178–194.

Lin, N. (1999). Building a network theory of social capital. *Connections, 22*(1), 28–51.

Marshall, M., & Stolle, D. (2004). Race and the city: Neighborhood context and the development of generalized trust. *Political Behavior, 26*(2), 126–153.

Mason, A. M., Drew, S., & Weaver, D. (2017). Managing crisis-induced uncertainty: First responder experiences from the 2011 Joplin-Duquesne tornado. *International Journal of Disaster Risk Reduction, 23*(August), 231–237.

Moran, P. (2005). Structural vs. relational embeddedness: Social capital and managerial performance. *Strategic Management Journal, 26*(12), 1129–1151.

Morrison, K. (2010). Complexity theory, school leadership and management: Questions for theory and practice. *Educational Management Administration and Leadership, 38*(4), 374–393.

Nickerson, D. W. (2009). Experimental approaches to the diffusion of norms. In V. O. Bartkus & J. H. Davies (Eds.), *Socal capital: Reaching out, reaching in* (pp. 186–204). Cheltenham: Edward Elgar.

Putnam, R. (1993). The prosperous community: Social capital and public life. *The American Prospect, 4*(13), 35–42.

Putnam, R. (2000). *Bowling alone: The collapse and revival of American community.* New York, NY: Simon and Schuster.

Putnam, R. (2004). *Education, diversity, social cohesion and 'social capital.'* Dublin: OECD Education Ministers.

Ryu, S. (2017). To bond or to bridge? Contingent effects of managers' social capital on organizational performance. *American Review of Public Administration, 47*(4), 403–418. Retrieved from http://journals.sagepub.com/doi/abs/10.1177/0275074015598392?journalCode=arpb

Schon, D. A. (1987). *Educating the reflective practitioner: Toward a new design for teaching and learning in the professions.* San Francisco, CA: Jossey-Bass.

Solomon, R. C., & Flores, F. (2001). *Building trust in business, politics, relationships, and life.* New York, NY: Oxford University Press.

Soltis, J. F. (1987). *Reforming teacher education: The impact of the Holmes group report.* New York, NY: Teachers College Press, Columbia University.

Sutherland, I. E. (2017). Learning and growing:Trust, leadership, and response to crisis. *Journal of Educational Administration, 55*(1), 2–17.

Tingley, S. (1996). Pooling our resources: Why are there so few candidates for superintendents? Maybe we are looking in the wrong places. *Education Week, Commentary, 16*(9), 38, 48.

Tsang, K.-K. (2010). School social capital and school effectiveness. *Education Journal, 37*(1–2), 119–136.

Tschannen-Moran, M. (2014). The interconnectivity of trust in schools. In D. V. Maele, P. B. Forsyth, & M. Van Houtte (Eds.), *Trust in school life: The role of trust for learning, teaching, leading, and bridging* (pp. 57–82). Dordecht: Springer.

Tschannen-Moran, M., & Hoy, W. K. (1998). Trust in schools: A conceptual and empirical analysis. *Journal of Educational Administration, 36*(4), 334–352.

Uhl-Bien, M. (2012). *Complexity leadership in healthcare organizations.* Retrieved from http://c.ymcdn.com/sites/www.plexusinstitute.org/resource/resmgr/files/complexity_leadership_plexus.pdf

Uhl-Bien, M., Marion, R., & McKelvey, B. (2007). Complexity leadership theory: Shifting leadership from the industrial age to the knowledge era. *The Leadership Quarterly, 18*(4), 298–318.

Ulmer, R. R., Sellnow, T. L., & Seeger, M. W. (2013). *Effective crisis communication: Moving from crisis to opportunity.* New York, NY: Sage Publications.

Van Lange, P. A. M., Rockenbach, B., & Yamagishi, T. (Eds.). (2017). *Trust in social dilemmas.* New York, NY: Oxford University Press.

Woolcock, M. (2001). The place of social capital in understanding social and economic outcomes. *Canadian Journal of Policy Research, 2*(1), 11–17.

CHAPTER 3

Making Sense of Uncertainty

In our discussion of networks, norms, and trust, we indicated that these play an important role in the amount of social capital educational leaders can draw upon in educational settings, especially when they are confronting the uncertainty inherent in complex problems, dilemmas, and crises. Whatever the nature of that uncertainty, however, we need to address it by making sense of what happens and by developing a plan for moving forward. In this chapter, we begin by exploring sensemaking (Weick, 1995) and related visualization tools, such as network pictures and relationship maps, that can enhance our understanding of leadership challenges and suggest ways to respond to them. Then, drawing from sensemaking, complex adaptive systems theory, complexity leadership theory, and social capital, we introduce a 5-step sensemaking approach that we think educational leaders will find very helpful in addressing the uncertainties they face.

1 Sensemaking

Much has been written about sensemaking since the term was first formally coined by Karl Weick (1995) in *Sensemaking in Organizations*. In that book, Weick refers to sensemaking as a perspective and states that "it is tested to the extreme when people encounter an event, the occurrence of which is so implausible that people don't believe what they are seeing" (Weick, 1995, p. 1). Maitlis and Christianson (2014) describe sensemaking as "the process through which individuals work to understand novel, unexpected,or confusing events" (p. 58). Over the years, the use of sensemaking to understand complex problems in organizations has grown exponentially with some scholars referring to the term as a "theory" (Holt & Cornelissen, 2013), some describing it as a "framework" (Mikkelsen, 2013), and others maintaining that sensemaking is a "lens" (Sonenshein, 2010; Stensaker & Falkenberg, 2007). Weick (1995) is unequivocal in stating that sensemaking is definitely not a theory. In his words, "there is no such thing as a theory of organizations that is characteristic of the sensemaking paradigm" (p. 69). For some, sensemaking is largely a cognitive process (Starbuck & Milliken, 1988) whereas for others, such as Maitlis and Christianson (2014), "it is much more common to find sensemaking framed as a social process because, even if individuals make sense on their own, they are embedded in a socio-material context" (p. 66). Combining these two schools of thought, we think of sensemaking as a social psychological process or what Berger and Luckmann (1966) describe as a process of social construction which involves individuals "placing bets" on what is going on during times of uncertainty and ambiguity. For our purposes, then, sensemaking is best thought of as an approach or a perspective one can take to navigate the dilemmas that arise in complex adaptive systems.

2   Properties of Sensemaking

Weick (1995) describes seven interconnected properties or characteristics of sensemaking which have been widely adopted (Colville & Pye, 2010; Currie & Brown, 2003; Thurlow & Mills, 2009). Broadly speaking, sensemaking,

- relates to identity
- is both retrospective and prospective
- involves enactment in some way
- is a social process
- is ongoing
- requires taking note of social cues
- values plausibility over certainty

The first of these, identity, is an important feature of sensemaking because as we try to make sense of the complex leadership challenges we face, we do so from our own experiences and our own personal histories. Those experiences and histories shape our personal and professional identities and inevitably, they affect how we interpret the challenges that we face as educational leaders (Thurlow & Mills, 2009; Watson, 2009).

Sensemaking also involves retrospection in that we shape experience into meaningful patterns according to our cumulative experiences over time (Weick, 1995). In other words, the process involves extracting cues and making plausible sense by looking backwards at what has happened between actors, why it has happened, and why it matters (Weick, Sutcliffe, & Obstfeld, 2005). Weick (1995) points out that sensemaking is also prospective in that it constructs an interpretation of reality so that some future action can be taken (Bruner, 1990; Currie & Brown, 2003; Watson, 1998). The act of speaking and building narrative accounts helps people to understand what they think, organize their experiences, control and predict future events, and reduce complexity (Abolifia, 2010; Isabella, 1990; Weick, 1995).

Even though sensemaking is enacted at the individual level, it is a social process which inevitably involves others. As educational leaders who operate in a continually dynamic environment, we need to understand how our actions and the actions of those in our bonding and bridging networks affect others. As Weick and Roberts (1993) suggest, sensemaking involves "a collective mind which is conceptualized as patterns of heedful interrelations of actions in a social system" (p. 357). The word "heedful" is particularly noteworthy in that it conjures images of leaders being mindful, attentive, and deliberate.

As Thurlow and Mills (2009) suggest, sensemaking involves individuals simultaneously shaping and reacting to the social environments they face. This is an ongoing, recursive process in which individuals adapt their identity based on how others behave toward them while simultaneously trying to influence the behaviour of others. It is this two-way process that perhaps best captures the dynamic and fluid nature of sensemaking.

Taking a sensemaking perspective involves picking up on social cues such as the assumptions people appear to be making, the emotions they are showing, and whether they are upholding or violating social norms. Using social cues, educational leaders can decide what needs attention and what does not. Over time, social cues can serve as important reference points for what may be happening and what actions may be needed in the future.

Finally, sensemaking helps us determine which account of events seems most likely; however, as Weick (1995) states, complete certainty is never possible within complex social processes:

> ...in an equivocal, postmodern world, infused with the politics of interpretation and conflicting interests and inhabited by people with multiple shifting identities, an obsession with accuracy seems fruitless, and not of much practical help, either. (p. 61)

As we have previously pointed out, these seven properties are interrelated and serve to help us make sense of complex challenges in educational settings through both our written and spoken narratives (Currie & Brown, 2003). Some of these challenges are more likely than others to trigger the need to engage in sensemaking in the first place.

3   Triggers for Sensemaking

As mentioned earlier, when the U.K. unexpectedly voted to leave the European
Union and the United States elected Donald Trump as President in 2016, these
startling results at the polls created widespread uncertainty. Such uncertainty
can be pervasive and affect our daily lives, but it is the complex problems
or intractable dilemmas that play out closer to home in our educational
institutions that are most likely to prompt us to take a sensemaking perspective.
Adaptive challenges or those which require effortful change can create a
disconnect between what we expect will happen and what actually happens.
Consequently, we may "suddenly and deeply feel that the universe is no longer
a rational, orderly system" (Weick, 1993, p. 633). Maitlis and Christianson
(2014) identify the three most commonly cited triggers for sensemaking as:
(1) environmental jolts and organizational crises, (2) threats to identity, and
(3) planned change interventions.

Environmental jolts occur in times of uncertainty when changes in the
external environment disrupt our ability to operate normally and challenge
our organizational routines (Daft & Weick, 1984). For example, the volatility of
an unexpected strike can trigger sensemaking not only among those who go on
strike but also among those who are left behind to try to carry on with business
as usual during the labour disruption. Moreover, when the labour disruption
ends, the work environment seldom returns to the state of equilibrium that
existed before the disruption. Tensions between those who participated
in the work stoppage and those who didn't, as well as continuing tensions
between management and labour, have the power to change an organization's
institutional norms and damage trust relationships between its members.
Using a sensemaking approach can help educational leaders retain a sense of
perspective about the sources of tensions in their institutions.

Organizational crises tend to have a broader impact than environmental jolts
and have the effect of "disrupting a wide range of existing understandings and
driving an intense and urgent search for explanations and appropriate courses
of action" (Pearson & Clair, 1998; Turner, 1976; Weick, 1993). In cases such as
public inquiries into wrongdoing in the private sector, within government, or
in medical fields, sensemaking can play a role not only after the fact but also
while the crisis is actually unfolding (Christianson, Farkas, Sutcliffe, & Weick,
2009; Weick, 1995).

Threats to identity trigger sensemaking when unforeseen experiences or
events call into question how people think of themselves both personally and
professionally. For example, when a faculty or school decides to discontinue a
program, those who were known as the "architects" of the program are often

left wondering "who they are" as professionals once the program no longer exists. Another example of threats to identity occurs when the rankings of schools are published in local newspapers and teachers suddenly learn that their schools are not considered to be performing as well as they had long thought. The expected response from teachers and staff can be one of disbelief, disorientation, and confusion when their long-held perceptions and reality collide. A sensemaking perspective can help to restore equilibrium and suggest plans for appropriate responses.

Although the first two triggers for sensemaking described by Maitlis and Christianson (2014) are generally unexpected, sensemaking can also be triggered by changes that are anticipated and planned. For example, many educational reforms, despite years of planning and preparation, nevertheless create so much disequilibrium that institutions often find themselves at the edge of chaos during the implementation period (Fullan, 2001). Although staff may have agreed to a planned change in the beginning, when reality sets in, there may be resentment or even resistance as the full implications of the change become apparent. Both leaders and followers may feel the need to take a sensemaking approach when this happens.

These three triggers provide useful touchstones for thinking about how complex problems arise in the first place and how they affect social networks. However promising sensemaking may be, educational leaders might still find this approach too theoretical when it comes to responding to challenges in their workplace. We argue that practical visualization tools such as network pictures and relationship maps can help make the abstract more concrete so we include these as part of our 5-step sensemaking approach.

4 Tools for Sensemaking

4.1 Network Pictures

The term *network pictures* is attributed to Asch's (1952) thinking about "activity systems" in the field of industrial marketing research in the early 2000s (Borders, Johnston, & Rigdon, 2001; Ford, Gadde, Hakansson, & Snehota, 2002). Although educational leaders seldom access this type of research, there are good reasons why they should. Network pictures can help educational leaders make sense of their bonding and bridging networks by actually mapping them out. According to Henneberg and Mouzas (2006),

> ...network pictures are managers' subjective mental representations of their relevant business environment. They are posited to work as

'sensemaking' devices and consequently, shape managerial decisions, actions, and evaluations...Inherent in these network pictures are managers' understandings of relationships, interactions and independencies. (pp. 408–409)

Consistent with the properties of sensemaking we have already discussed, network pictures are both retrospective, in that they portray one's understanding of what has happened both in the past and in the present, and prospective, in that they provide direction for the future. In other words, network pictures are highly subjective in nature or as Henneberg and Mouzas (2006) point out, "they are not objectively given but socially constructed, a bounded, personal interpretation of the network context" and therefore, "determined in a purely individual way" (p. 410).

An example of a network picture that was drawn from the perspective of a superintendent of schools is presented in Figure 3.1.

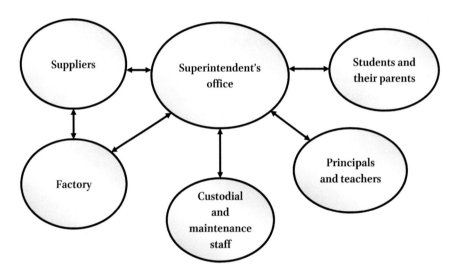

FIGURE 3.1   *Example of a network picture*

We can see at a glance that the superintendent must interact with a wide variety of networks, each with their own priorities and agendas. Even this simple network picture can help an educational leader make sense of how complex problems can impact one or more of these interconnected networks. Consider the problem of ensuring that all schools in the district are fully equipped on the first day of school. The superintendent's office must be in constant communication with suppliers of everything from paper and pencils to copy machines and classroom furniture. At times, the superintendent's office might even need to communicate with the factories to ensure that supplies reach schools on time. On the receiving end are students and their parents as well as principals and teachers who need all kinds of supplies in order to do their work. Furthermore, custodial and maintenance staff, who are responsible for stocking, loading, cleaning, and repairing are also affected when supplies purchased for the school are not available as promised.

We think that the simple network picture in Figure 3.1 illustrates several important points about sensemaking devices in general:

– they are subjective portrayals of one person's perspective;
– they focus on networks of people and not on individuals; and,
– they illustrate whether the interactions between networks are one-way or two-way in nature.

4.2   Relationship Maps

Although network pictures have value, we think that *relationship maps* (Sutcliffe, 2008) are even more useful in distinguishing between basic problems and more challenging dilemmas and as such, they play an important role in the 5-step sensemaking approach we describe in the remainder of this chapter. To understand the distinction between these two visualization tools, it is helpful to point out the similarities and differences between network pictures and relationship maps. First, they are both subjective visual representations of social networks and as such, they illustrate how various parties interact with one another and the ways in which they are interdependent. In fact, the visual aspect of both sensemaking devices underscores Weick's (1995) fundamental question which is, "How can I know what I think until I see what I say?" (p. 25). Second, both tools are retrospective and prospective at the same time; in other words, they require the individual drawing them to look back on a situation to enable them to look forward. Along with these similarities, however, we think that there are also some significant differences. First, relationship maps have their origins in educational settings rather than the business world and as most educators will be quick to point out, the fields of education and business are vastly different. Second, relationship maps tend to focus more on the micro level as opposed to network pictures which focus more on interactions at the macro level. Finally, and perhaps most importantly, relationship maps focus on the level of trust that exists between the actors in the network being examined.

Like the visualization of social networks in Sutcliffe's (2008) work, relationship maps consider the nature of trust between the individuals and whether they perceive trust to be symmetrical (two-way) or asymmetrical (one-way) in their networks. Rather than using Sutcliffe's terminology of "high, neutral, and distrust," however, as indicated in Chapter 2, we find the words, "provisional, profound, and broken" to be more descriptive. Relationship maps are also similar to conflict maps (Mason & Rychard, 2005) which represent "a specific view point (of the person or group who is mapping) of a specific conflict situation...at a specific moment in time, similar to a photograph" (p. 5). Both conflict maps and relationship maps simplify what happens and in so doing can serve to clarify relationships. Like Mason and Rychard (2005), we use circles to denote actors and arrows to indicate relationships. However, since our focus is on trust and not conflict, we use different types of one-way and two-way arrows. As Table 3.1 below illustrates, we create thick arrows to show profound trust, thin arrows for provisional trust, and dashed arrows to point to trust that is breaking down or has completely broken down.

TABLE 3.1   *Denoting levels of trust in relationships*

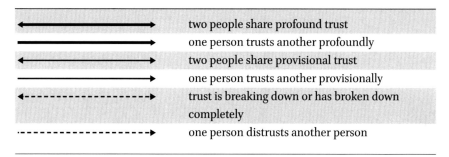

←——————————→	two people share profound trust
——————————→	one person trusts another profoundly
←——————————→	two people share provisional trust
——————————→	one person trusts another provisionally
←- - - - - - - - - - - -→	trust is breaking down or has broken down completely
· - - - - - - - - - - - -→	one person distrusts another person

Below, we illustrate what a relationship map might look like for the same superintendent, featured in the network picture (Figure 3.1) when he is faced with a dilemma. But first, some additional details are necessary. The superintendent, Lester McWilliams, has had a disturbing conversation with the Director of Maintenance, Sheryl Kouzac. Sheryl and Lester had worked closely for over 15 years and had developed a shared vision of how the district office should operate. They knew they could always count on one another to be honest and fair. Lester asked Sheryl about the paper products being supplied from Wyndham Industries. He had numerous complaints from principals who claimed that the products were inferior and in some cases, unusable. As he talked about the situation with Sheryl, he discovered that she was already investigating a worrying trend in the Wyndham Industries' accounts that pointed to some possible mismanagement by Carla Petrowski, Jake Halbersham's sister. When a sudden vacancy came up in Sheryl's office about a year ago, Jake, who was the chairman of the Board of Trustees, had "suggested" that she hire Carla, who had just moved back to the community. Jake was a hard man to refuse. He was always ready to do anyone a favour and was a highly successful businessman who was fiercely loyal to his family and close friends. Unfortunately, Sheryl suspected that Carla and Martin Gislason, from Wyndham Industries were skimming off the top and providing cheaper, poorer quality paper products to the district's schools. As Sheryl and Lester reviewed the evidence they became increasingly alarmed about the implications of the situation they were now forced to address. A relationship map drawn from Lester's point of view might look like Figure 3.2.

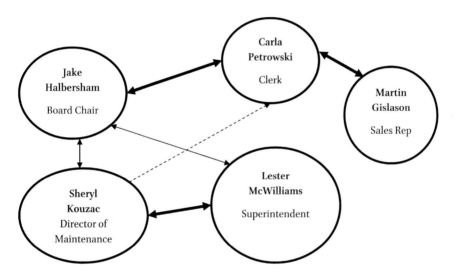

FIGURE 3.2   *Example of a relationship map*

   Our experience, and those of our interviewees, suggests that applying relationship mapping to complex problems or dilemmas as part of the sensemaking approach generates deeper and clearer insights and maintains our focus on what is most important. Therefore, we have incorporated relationship maps as an important step in the 5-step sensemaking approach we have developed for educational leaders. We outline this approach in Table 3.2 that educational leaders can use to navigate the complex adaptive systems in which they work.

TABLE 3.2   *The 5-step sensemaking approach at a glance*

Step 1: What is going on here?
Zero in on the problem or dilemma you need to address by answering the following
question: *What incident or situation precipitated this problem or dilemma?*

Step 2: Who is involved?
Determine who is directly or indirectly involved and draw a circle for each, keeping
in mind how each person is related to one another in the organizational hierarchy.
Label each circle.

Step 3: What do the relationships look like?
Connect each circle with one of the following three types of lines to create a
relationship map that shows what level of trust you think characterizes each
relationship:

- thick line ━━━━━ signifies relationships where there is profound trust
- thin line ────── indicates relationships where there is provisional trust
- dashed line -------- identifies relationships in which trust is breaking down or
  has broken down completely.

Complete the map by placing arrows at the ends of each line, to indicate whether
the trust in this relationship is one-way or reciprocal.

Step 4: What do I know for certain? What do I still need to know?
Use the Certainty Matrix as a guide to answer the following questions about what
you know about the incident or situation and how you know it:
- What do I know?
- What do I think I know?
- What don't I know?
- What ought I to know?

Step 5: What are my next steps?
Lay out your options and then use the following criteria as a guide for selecting the
best way forward:
- Will the norms of the institution be upheld or violated?
- Will network ties be strengthened or weakened?
- Will trust be deepened or damaged?
- Will we be closer to equilibrium?

We now turn to a real-life example of a relationship challenge faced by Travis Elliot, a newly hired vice-principal in a large urban school. Following the scenario, we learn how Travis makes sense of the challenges he faces by using the 5-step sensemaking approach.

5   The Revolving Door

Based on his record of building positive school climate in a number of high-needs schools in the area, Travis Elliott was recruited to replace Marilyn Desoto, as one of three vice-principals at Elmgrove High. Like a number of others on the senior leadership team, Marilyn had left for what was euphemistically being called "mental health" reasons. The general consensus was that Marilyn had left as a result of her principal, Holly Teasdale, whose inability to delegate and her lack of attention to building and sustaining trusting relationships had infuriated Marilyn. Travis knew that Holly had already been principal at Elmgrove for five years, but what he didn't realize until he began work at the school was how many changes there had been in the senior leadership team during that time.

At his first meeting with Jurgen Reis, the Director of Student Support Services, Travis got an earful. Jurgen was also threatening to leave because, as he explained to Travis, he and many other members of the senior leadership team felt smothered by Holly's need to know every detail of every project. Her demanding attitude and dismissive manner did not help matters much either.

Travis got a very different perspective from Tanis Courchaine, who was new to educational leadership, but had known Holly for many years as a staff member. As a vice-principal, Tanis had been immediately taken into Holly's confidence and perhaps that was why she spoke so glowingly of Holly and her leadership of the school. Some mockingly said that the two women "were joined at the hip."

Max Robarts, the third and longest serving vice-principal, tried to ignore what was going on in the office and seemed to be marking time until his upcoming retirement. He couldn't hide his body language, however, which showed that he was highly disapproving of Holly's management style.

The school board attributed the steady turnover of staff to the heavy workload of a large institution. In fact, the trustees had recently voted, on Holly's recommendation, to hire a fourth vice principal. They also decided that once this position was filled that each staff member, including members of the senior leadership team, would report to one of the four vice-principals and that only the vice-principals would report directly to Holly.

Travis was determined to develop a more positive working environment in which everyone who reported to him was recognized as a valued team member. Nevertheless, he suspected that it would take more than shuffling the organizational chart and adding a new position to change Holly's behaviour and restore the equilibrium of the school. Somehow, Travis would have to find a way to develop a trusting relationship with Holly or it wouldn't be long before he, too, followed the others through the revolving door.

6   Travis Elliott Applies the 5-Step Sensemaking Approach

Step 1: What is going on here?
I am joining a leadership team in which it appears that the leader has dysfunctional relationships with the other members of the leadership team. My sense is that hiring a fourth vice-principal will not change Holly's difficult behaviour, but I have to be open to the possibility that it might make a difference. It seems as though Holly has been intentionally or unintentionally sabotaging the authority of those who work most closely with her by failing to trust anyone else.

Step 2: Who is involved?
Although Holly's behaviour affects almost everyone in the school to some degree, the people most directly involved in my dilemma in addition to her are the other vice-principals, Tanis Courchaine and Max Robarts, Jurgen Reis, the school's Director of Student Services, and the trustees of the school district.

Step 3: What do the relationships look like?
Looking at my relationship map, Holly appears to have profound trust in Tanis but she does not seem to have trusting relationships with anyone else on staff, and for some, like Jurgen and Max, trust has completely broken down. I need to try not to be swayed by what has happened in the past and give Holly a chance to step back and implement the board's reorganization plan. The trustees must still have profound trust in Holly or they wouldn't have accepted her recommendation to hire a fourth vice-principal. Based on my experiences in other schools, I am confident that I can develop provisional trust with all those who report to me and eventually profound trust with some.

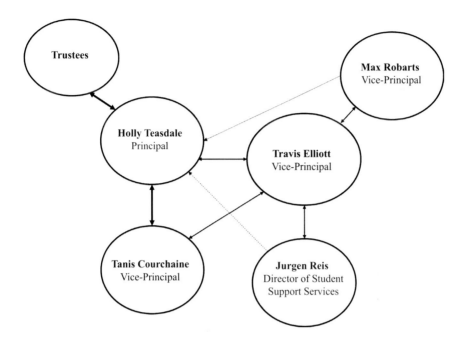

FIGURE 3.3   *Travis's relationship map (The Revolving Door)*

Step 4: What do I know for certain? What do I still need to know?
I am facing a number of unknowns in this situation so it would be helpful to use a Certainty Matrix (Table 3.3) to sort through what and who I can count on as I start my new position.

Step 5: What are my next steps?
I will need to have a substantive yet respectful conversation with Holly about her leadership style, her expectations for me, and the degree of oversight that I can expect. I will need to do so in a way that doesn't threaten her, but actually begins the trust building process. It would be helpful for me to have a window into the norms of the school and the leadership team, at least from Holly's perspective. Once I know who is reporting directly to me, I will need to establish our norms of collaboration. As we frame our work together, I need to ensure that our conversations are not perceived as an opportunity to gripe about Holly. After all, the last thing that I want is to have Holly think that I am trying to weaken network ties, damage trust, or cause disequilibrium within the school. I may need to draw on the social capital I have already accrued from my other professional networks to help me tackle the dysfunctional leadership in this school.

TABLE 3.3   *Travis's Certainty Matrix (The Revolving Door)*

	Certainties	Uncertainties
Warranted	*I know...* – that Jurgen has threatened to leave. – that one vice-principal has left for "mental health reasons." – one vice-principal has retreated into "on the job retirement." – that the trustees have decided to hire a fourth vice-principal. – that some directors and teachers are being reassigned to report to me.	*I don't know...* – if what others say about Holly is actually true. – if Holly will try to micromanage me. – if I understand the context accurately. – if I can break through the climate of distrust and build trusting relationships with those who report to me. – if I can remain open-minded.
Unwarranted	*I think I know...* – that building a trusting relationship with Holly will be challenging. – that Tanis will always support Holly, no matter what. – that the board is prepared to continue to support Holly.	*I ought to know...* – whether staff were honest about why they were leaving in their exit interviews. – whether rumours about why Marilyn Desoto really left are actually true. – how Tanis manages to maintain such a close relationship with Holly.

For Travis and other educational leaders using the 5-step sensemaking approach, the real benefit is in going through the steps to gain insight into the context, players, and consequences of the actions one might take. It is deliberately constructed, not as a recipe for solving dilemmas, but for thinking more deeply about them.

I guess it isn't surprising that my relationship map is messy because quite frankly, leading is messy. (Dean)

In the next chapter, we present three scenarios that illustrate very different dilemmas that are experienced by a principal, a superintendent, and a dean of education. As we have just done with *The Revolving Door,* we will provide an extensive narrative to show how an educational leader might use the 5-step sensemaking approach to think through the complex problems he or she faces.

References

Abolifia, M. Y. (2010). Narrative construction in sensemaking: How a central bank thinks. *Organization Studies, 31*(3), 349–367.

Asch, S. E. (1952). *Social psychology.* Englewood Cliffs, NJ: Prentice-Hall.

Berger, P., & Luckmann, T. (1966). *The social construction of reality: A treatise in the sociology of knowledge.* London: Penguin Books.

Borders, A. L., Johnston, W. J., & Rigdon, E. E. (2001). Beyond the dyad: Electronic commerce and network perspectives in industrial marketing management. *Industrial Marketing Management, 30,* 199–205.

Bruner, J. (1990). *Acts of meaning.* Cambridge, MA: Harvard University Press.

Christianson, M. K., Farkas, M. T., Sutcliffe, K. M., & Weick, K. E. (2009). Learning through rare events: Significant interruptions at the Baltimore & Ohio Railroad Museum. *Organizational Science, 20*(5), 846–860.

Colville, I., & Pye, A. (2010). A sensemaking perspective on network pictures. *Industrial Marketing Management, 39,* 372–380.

Currie, G., & Brown, A. D. (2003). A narratological approach to understanding processes of organizing in a UK hospital. *Human Relations, 56*(5), 563–586.

Daft, R. L., & Weick, K. E. (1984). Toward a model of organizations as interpretation systems. *Academy of Management Review, 9*(2), 284–295.

Ford, D., Gadde, L.-E., Hakansson, H., & Snehota, I. (2002). *Managing networks.* Paper presented at the IMP Conference, Perth, Australia.

Fullan, M. (2001). *Leading in a culture of change.* San Francisco, CA: Jossey-Bass.

Henneberg, S. C., & Mouzas, S. (2006). Network pictures: Concepts and representations *European Journal of Marketing, 40*(3–4), 408–429.

Holt, R., & Cornelissen, J. (2013). Sensemaking revisited. *Management Learning, 45*(5), 525–539.

Isabella, L. A. (1990). Evolving interpretations as a change unfolds: How managers construe key organizational events. *Academy of Management Journal, 56*(1), 7–41.

Maitlis, S., & Christianson, M. (2014). Sensemaking in organizations: Taking stock and moving forward. *The Academy of Management Annals, 8*(1), 57–125.

Mason, S., & Rychard, S. (2005). *Conflict analysis tools*. Retrieved from
    http://www.css.ethz.ch/en/center/people/mason-simon-all-publications/
    details.html?id=/c/o/n/f/conflict_analysis_tools

Mikkelsen, E. N. (2013). A researcher's tale: How doing conflict research shapes
    research about conflict. *Qualitative Research in Organizations and Management:
    An International Journal, 8*(1), 33–49.

Pearson, C. M., & Clair, J. A. (1998). Reframing crisis management. *Academy of
    Management Review, 23*(1), 59–76.

Sonenshein, S. (2010). We're changing or are we? Untangling the role of progressive,
    regressive, and stability narratives during strategic change implementation.
    Academy of Management Journal, 53(3), 477–512.

Starbuck, W. H., & Milliken, F. J. (1988). Executives' perceptual filters: What they notice
    and how they make sense. In D. C. Hambrick (Ed.), *The executive effect: Concepts and
    methods for studying top managers* (pp. 35–65). Greenwich, CT: JAI Press.

Stensaker, I., & Falkenberg, J. (2007). Making sense of different responses to corporate
    change. *Human Relations, 60*(1), 137–177.

Sutcliffe, A. (2008). A design framework for mapping social relationships. *PsychNology
    Journal, 6*(3), 225–246.

Thurlow, A., & Mills, J. H. (2009). Change, talk and sensemaking. *Journal of
    Organizational Change Management, 22*(5), 459–479.

Turner, B. (1976). The organizational and interorganizational development of disasters.
    Administrative Science Quarterly, 21(3), 378–397.

Watson, T. J. (1998). Managerial sensemaking and occupational identities in Britain and
    Italy: The role of management magazines in the process of discursive construction.
    Journal of Management Studies, 35(3), 285–301.

Watson, T. J. (2009). Narrative life story and the management of identity: A case study
    in autobiographical identity work. *Human Relations, 62*(3), 1–28.

Weick, K. E. (1993). The collapse of sensemaking in organizations: The Mann Gulch
    disaster. *Administrative Science Quarterly, 38*(4), 628–652.

Weick, K. E. (1995). *Sensemaking in organizations*. Thousand Oaks, CA: Sage
    Publications.

Weick, K. E., & Roberts, K. H. (1993). Collective mind in organizations: Heedful
    interrelating on flight decks. *Administrative Science Quarterly, 38*(3), 357–381.

Weick, K. E., Sutcliffe, K. M., & Obstfeld, D. (2005). Organizing and the process of
    sensemaking. *Organizational Science, 16*(4), 409–421.

CHAPTER 4

Grappling with Uncertainty

1   Modeling the 5-Step Sensemaking Approach

Now that we have provided the background for the 5-step sensemaking approach and outlined its features, we present three scenarios to demonstrate how it can be applied by different educational leaders. Although we frame each scenario as occurring in a specific educational setting, the challenging situation that arises to test these educational leaders is not exclusive to that setting. Indeed, educational institutions are all complex adaptive systems and as such, leadership challenges, especially those related to relationships and authority, are essentially the same whether the setting is a school, a district office, or a faculty of education. In other words, we have chosen these scenarios with the idea that readers can relate to the dilemmas we depict rather than focus on how the setting or role of the educational leader is different from their own. After each scenario, we walk through the 5-step sensemaking approach as if we were the educational leader involved and make reference to themes and concepts we explored earlier in the book.

The first scenario features a perplexing human resource issue in which a principal, Scott Davis, is trying to make sense of who he can trust.

2   Benefit of the Doubt

Charlene Miller and Doug Freeman were long-time teaching partners at a large suburban high school in a mid-western city who were jokingly said to be "in each other's pocket." It seemed as if they were always together and held similar strong opinions. In spite of the fact that their first point of call should have been Freya McAllister, the senior vice-principal, they decided to go directly to their principal, Scott Davis, with their latest concerns about their colleague, Heather Heleyar. Like others on staff, they knew that Heather was experiencing marital problems and were aware that she seemed distracted, but Charlene and Doug also believed that she was becoming increasingly suspicious of others' intentions. As principal, Scott had been trying to support Heather and he had already suggested that she seek counseling and even consider going on medical leave. However, Heather remained adamant that she could handle things on her own.

© KONINKLIJKE BRILL NV, LEIDEN, 2018 | DOI 10.1163/9789004368484_004

Scott was surprised when Charlene and Doug asked to meet him in the park across from the school to talk about Heather, but he reluctantly agreed to the meeting. Seconds into their conversation, Charlene told Scott that he shouldn't breathe a word of this meeting to Freya. Doug immediately chimed in that they were coming to him because they knew Freya wouldn't take their concerns about Heather seriously. Charlene agreed and went on to complain that Freya was indifferent to Heather's problems.

Scott knew that like any leader, Freya wasn't perfect, but he also knew that she had been reaching out regularly to Heather, checking in on her periodically, and even taking her out for coffee from time to time. Consequently, he told Charlene and Doug that he wasn't prepared to keep this conversation a secret from Freya. For one thing, Scott was not about to jeopardize either the trust he and Freya had been working so hard to develop or risk loosening the ties in his administrative team. Charlene and Doug were clearly disappointed with his response, but they nevertheless managed to keep him captive for another half an hour relating what they said they "knew" about Heather's state of mind and her erratic behavior.

Although Scott had to admit there was a real possibility that Charlene and Doug had Heather's interests genuinely at heart, as far as he knew, they had very little to do with each other as colleagues, inside or outside of school. He wondered where this newfound interest in Heather had anything to do with Charlene's not so hidden desire to become an administrator. In fact, Scott found both of them to be very difficult to deal with because they seemed to be continually encouraging staff to follow their lead on whatever "project" that had recently grabbed their attention without going through the appropriate channels. Scott was fairly certain that Heather was simply another one of their short-lived enthusiasms. In this case, however, their interference involved a highly sensitive personnel matter and could negatively affect Heather's ability to cope.

Nevertheless, as he drove home that night, he found himself going back and forth between giving Charlene and Doug the benefit of the doubt and thinking that their real agenda was simply to look as if they, and not Scott or Freya, were the real leaders of the school. His instincts told him to proceed with caution and to maintain his focus on finding ways for the school to come together to support Heather during these challenging times.

Scott is confronting a dilemma that most of us face throughout our professional lives, that is, deciding who to trust and then trying to determine just how much we can trust them. Scott decides to tackle this question by working through the 5-step sensemaking approach to organize his thoughts. Here's what the approach looks like from Scott's perspective:

3   Scott Davis Applies the 5-Step Sensemaking Approach

Step 1: What is going on here?
Heather Heleyar is undergoing a stressful time in her life and it appears as though her personal problems have become a "project" for Charlene Miller and Doug Freeman, who see themselves as emergent leaders. In this instance, they have decided to go around the senior vice-principal, Freya McAllister, and have approached me to meet outside of school to discuss Heather's needs. They have complained that Freya is indifferent to Heather's situation and have taken it upon themselves to speak on Heather's behalf.

Step 2: Who is involved?
Apart from me, the most directly involved in this situation are Charlene and Doug, their struggling colleague, Heather, and Freya, who Charlene and Doug are trying to by-pass.

Step 3: What do the relationships look like?
Drawing a relationship map helps me to think more deeply about what is going on between the individuals who are involved. There is clearly profound trust between Charlene and Doug, who are deeply entangled in each other's lives. For my part, I feel able to trust them only provisionally, based on their frequent attempts to circumvent formal authority and exert their own authority as informal leaders. Meanwhile, I want to be careful that I am not making unfair assumptions about their motivations. At this point, my relationship with Freya is provisionally trusting, but we are both working hard to build and sustain a more profoundly trusting relationship. The harder question is what kind of relationships Heather has with the rest of us. According to Charlene and Doug, at least, she has become suspicious of everyone. I personally don't see that Heather's relationships have generally broken down with other members of staff but Charlene and Doug have raised this as an issue.

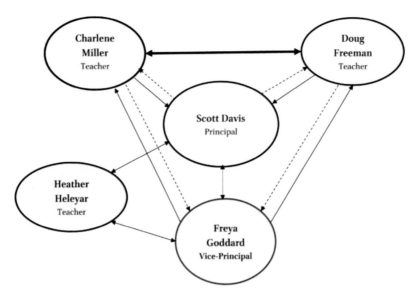

FIGURE 4.1   *Scott's relationship map* (*Benefit of the Doubt*)

Step 4: What do I know for certain? What do I still need to know?
Completing a Certainty Matrix will help me sort out what I know for sure and what I am still wondering about.

Step 5: What are my next steps?
Thinking about what I have entered into the Certainty Matrix, I have a better idea of what I know for certain and what I still need to know. I still need to get to the bottom of why Charlene and Doug felt it was so important that they meet me away from the school. Such meetings violate the norms of openness and trust that we have worked so hard to establish for all of our social networks in the school. I also need to find out why they wanted me to keep our conversation a secret from Freya. This is not the first time that Charlene and Doug have tried to by-pass the conventional authority structures in the school and unless the administrative team addresses this, we may find ourselves heading toward the edge of chaos. That's why I knew that I couldn't ignore their attempt to cut Freya out of the loop. Whatever I decide to do, I want to reinforce the norms of trust in the school and not inadvertently weaken ties between people.

First and foremost, I need to focus my attention on Heather and the welfare of her students. I have not had any complaints from parents or students, but it may be worthwhile to include Heather's classes more intentionally in my "walk-throughs" to get a sense of what is happening there. I think I should ask

TABLE 4.1   *Scott's Certainty Matrix (Benefit of the Doubt)*

	Certainties	Uncertainties
Warranted	*I know...* – that Heather is struggling and needs support from people she can trust – that Freya has been reaching out to Heather – that Charlene and Doug claim that Freya is indifferent to Heather's situation – that Charlene and Doug claim that Heather is increasingly suspicious of others' intentions – that I need to sustain trust with Freya and the rest of the administrative team	*I don't know...* – if Charlene and Doug really have Heather's best interests in mind – whether Charlene and Doug's actions will negatively affect Heather – how well Heather is actually coping
Unwarranted	*I think I know...* – why Charlene and Doug have adopted Heather as their latest "project" – why Charlene and Doug are keeping Freya in the dark	*I ought to know...* – why Charlene and Doug wanted to meet me outside of the school – what the shared history is between Charlene and Doug and Heather – whether there is a hidden agenda underlying Charlene and Doug's actions

Heather about the nature of her relationships with Charlene and Doug. She can tell me whether they are as close to her as they would have me believe. If not, I can discount their claims about Heather's state of mind and behavior. In that case, I can chalk this up as yet another attempt to demonstrate that as informal leaders, they are doing what the formal administration is failing to do. Once I brief Freya on what has happened, together, we can lay out the situation for the whole administrative team so we can decide how best to deal with Charlene and Doug's attempts to undermine the authority of designated leaders and think of additional ways we can support Heather as she deals with her problems.

We turn now to the case of a school superintendent who is faced with a challenge that pits personal allegiance against the need for leadership renewal at the institutional level.

4   No Easy Answers

Henry Wall was a newly-appointed school superintendent who had spent the past eight years as one of two assistant superintendents in a relatively small rural school district. In these early days of being in his new position, Henry was preoccupied with many competing priorities, but none was more important than the one screaming at him from the memo in his hand. The Board had just announced devastating cuts that he would have to deal with immediately. For one thing, it meant that it would be impossible for him to add the third assistant superintendent that he had been promised when he was hired. Now he would be forced to completely rethink the composition of his leadership team.

Probably the person who would be most affected by this turn of events was his long-time colleague and close ally, Steve Stanton, who had been an assistant superintendent in the district for 23 years. Henry and Steve had served together as assistant superintendents for almost 10 years under the previous administration. They had been through many challenges together and in the process, they had come to depend upon each other, particularly when they were left in charge while the previous superintendent was engaged in external work. In spite of their shared history Henry had begun to wonder whether Steve had the fresh ideas and positive energy that the district needed at this time. Henry realized that he was making an assumption that Steve actually wanted to stay on and if he didn't, there were at least three other positions that he could think of that would be suitable for him. He was beginning to think that it was time for others to be given the opportunity.

In fact, there were two people, Sam Burns and Phyllis Grapelli, who were more than ready to step up and, on the Board's recommendation, Henry had already spoken with them about filling his position and the new one he had been promised. Both were highly respected and experienced school administrators who worked closely together and collaborated effectively on a number of diverse district projects. Now

Henry was faced with the awkward and difficult dilemma of having to choose only two assistant superintendents out of three highly-qualified people. How would he choose? If he followed his inclination and reassigned Steve or asked him to step down, he would certainly damage the trusting relationship that they had developed over the years and possibly do irreparable harm to his reputation. If he kept Steve because of his institutional knowledge and in deference to their many years of working together, he would have to break the promise he had made to Sam or Phyllis since he could only hire one of them. Henry wasn't exactly sure what he would do but he was certain that no matter what he decided, one of his valued colleagues was going to feel betrayed.

Like so many other educational leaders, Henry is faced with a dilemma that is not of his own making. He has no control over the sudden budget cuts or the effect they will have on his hiring decisions. Henry decides to use the 5-step sensemaking approach to clarify his options. Here is what the approach might actually look like as Henry works through it.

5   Henry Wall Applies the 5-Step Sensemaking Approach

Step 1: What is going on here?
Due to these unexpected budget cuts, I will have to make some hard decisions about who I want to be my assistant superintendents. I feel a strong sense of loyalty to Steve, but after 23 years as an assistant superintendent, it may be time for him to step aside and let someone else step in. However, I am concerned that if I re-assign Steve or ask him to step down, people will think that Steve isn't up to the job anymore, and that would be unfair. I am also distressed to think that I may have to choose between Sam and Phyllis who are equally qualified to serve and who had every reason to assume that they would be appointed to their new roles in the near future.

Step 2: Who is involved?
I think the people most directly involved besides me are Steve Stanton, the current assistant superintendent and my long-time colleague, two experienced school administrators, Phyllis Grapelli and Sam Burns, and the Board, which has just created this dilemma.

Step 3: What do the relationships look like?

I need to draw a relationship map so I can organize my thinking about the effect of this dilemma on the level of trust in my relationships. I know that the profound trust relationship I have with Steve is reciprocated. I am sure that this is the main reason why I am struggling so much with the idea of letting him go. If I do, I am quite sure that the trust between us will be damaged and will be very difficult, if not impossible, to repair. I know that Sam and Phyllis share a profound trust given their excitement about working together as assistant superintendents. As principals at neighboring schools, they have had many opportunities to build a strong relationship as they have worked collaboratively on joint projects and have served on many committees together. I also trust Sam and Phyllis completely; otherwise, I wouldn't have tapped them on the shoulder to be on the senior leadership team. I have every reason to believe that they feel the same way about me, but this will certainly change if I appoint one and not the other. I know that the Board trusts me deeply but I have to say that this bombshell has shaken my trust in them.

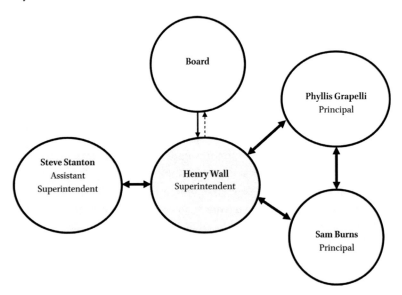

FIGURE 4.2   *Henry's relationship map (No Easy Answers)*

Step 4: What do I know for certain? What do I still need to know?

I think it would be helpful for me to complete a Certainty Matrix so that I can be as mindful as possible about the decision that I have been forced to make.

Step 5: What are my next steps?

I need to keep in mind how complex this situation really is if I want to uphold positive social norms, strengthen networks, deepen trust, and maintain the equilibrium of the senior leadership team. Looking at my completed Certainty Matrix, I realize that I have to engage Steve in a conversation about his professional aspirations. First, I will need to find out whether Steve might

TABLE 4.2   *Henry's Certainty Matrix (No Easy Answers)*

	Certainties	Uncertainties
Warranted	*I know...* – I need to completely re-think my plans for the senior leadership team – that Steve has been my trusted colleague for many years – I know that Phyllis and Sam work well together – that both Phyllis and Sam think they are both going to be assistant superintendents – that Phyllis and Sam are ready to take on the challenge – that one of the three is bound to be disappointed once I announce who my new appointee(s) will be	*I don't know...* – how Steve will feel if I tell him that his services are no longer needed in his current role – which of the three available administrative positions Steve might be interested in – how Phyllis and Sam are going to react if one of them isn't chosen – what the impact on the district will be if I ask Steve to step down
Unwarranted	*I think I know...* – how Steve will react if he is not re-appointed – what the optics might be if Steve is not re-appointed – what would be the best composition of the senior leadership team	*I ought to know...* – whether Steve even wants to continue in his current role – if there is a chance to reverse the Board's decision – why I wasn't included in the decision making – how to retain my colleagues' trust in light of the Board's decision

actually welcome a change at this point in his career. The important thing is that we need to have a frank conversation. I need to be up front with Steve about what I am thinking and Steve needs to be honest about how such a change might affect him personally and professionally. As a new superintendent, I need to learn why I wasn't consulted before the Board made its decision and whether there is a chance of reversing it. Finally, if I can't appoint Sam and Phyllis together, then which one will it be? If I have to turn one of them down after telling them that they will both get this promotion, it will certainly erode the trust that we currently share. I may not have created this dilemma but I am now burdened with the knowledge that I will inevitably lose the trust of valued colleagues no matter what I do.

We now turn our attention to a dean of education who is faced with a difficult administrative decision that will inevitably alienate some faculty members and support staff who may have initially supported her.

6   Dropping Enrolments

Erin Bruce was a dean of education in a mid-sized faculty of education with about 50 full-time faculty members at a large, comprehensive university. Over the past few years, Erin had noticed that enrolments in the foundations courses were dropping; in fact, class sizes had become so small in these courses that they were no longer financially viable. Erin knew that something had to be done, but she was reluctant to see the end of philosophy, sociology, and history of education courses in the faculty, which she had long considered to be an essential grounding for a teacher's preparation. Three years before, when she was first appointed dean, she had promised to support the foundations in spite of the fact that undergraduates were no longer required to take one foundation course in each year to graduate and fewer students were choosing these courses as electives. Erin discussed her observations and thoughts with her Provost, Janet Siegel, who was both her mentor and close friend. Janet helped Erin understand that she really had very little choice in the matter since the university was under financial constraint and the faculty of education was expected to do its part in eliminating redundancies. Erin reluctantly agreed with Janet, but she knew it would be challenging to convince some of her colleagues that this was the right decision.

Although she knew that she had the authority to make this decision on her own, Erin felt the need to consult with her Faculty Council before she made her final determination. She was especially concerned about her trusted colleagues, Marsha Wainwright and Greg Czorny. After all, they were the "architects" of the foundations programs and had been heavily invested in their delivery for many years. But she was also concerned about how other faculty would react if they thought that they would be expected to "shoehorn" foundations content into their courses.

As expected, consultations did not go well. Marsha and Greg, in particular, argued that the enrolment data that Erin had collected wasn't accurate. More importantly, they complained that Erin was failing to support the very courses students needed if they were ever going to "learn to think for themselves." Furthermore, they were shocked that these discussions had not considered the implications for graduate students who might need foundations courses as pre-requisites.

Before long, they were raising alarm bells with others, including members of the staff who had provided support to their courses and who were afraid that they would lose their jobs. One of those people, Sandra Sanchez, the senior academic advisor, was so upset by the prospect that she had already been in contact with her union representative. She asked what he could do to help them save their jobs from what she called, "a power hungry dean who had no regard for the people who kept the faculty and its courses running." In her heart, Erin believed in the value of the foundations courses and she hated being seen as going back on her word. However, she also knew that the Faculty could not continue to lose money on courses that were poorly subscribed. Given that all faculty members' jobs would be protected and that all staff would be re-assigned elsewhere in the university, Erin knew what she needed to do even if the trust that some had placed in her was about to be tested.

Educational institutions are complex adaptive systems in which no single part works in isolation. When financial restraints tighten in a university, every faculty is affected. Consequently, Erin is caught in a conflict between her role as a fiscally responsible member of the senior leadership team and her role as an educational leader in her faculty. She must do her part to rein in costs while trying to maintain the integrity of the program and the trust of those around her. Erin decides to use the 5-step sensemaking approach to clarify her position. Here is what it looks like as Erin works through it.

7   **Erin Bruce Applies the 5-Step Sensemaking Approach**

Step 1: What is going on here?
I can see that the foundations courses are no longer sustainable. However, I promised not to cut these courses and many faculty and staff members counted on me to keep that pledge. I am sure I will be perceived as doing an about-face and will be expected to justify why I am changing course.

Step 2: Who is involved?
In addition to me, the main people involved are Janet Siegel, my provost, faculty members Marsha Wainwright and Greg Czorny, who appear to be inflaming fears and anxiety among faculty members and support staff, and Sandra Sanchez, the senior academic advisor, who is vocal about the negative effect of the expected staffing changes.

Step 3: What do the relationships look like?
As I draw my relationship map, I can see that the decision that I am about to make will exacerbate an already inflamed situation. I know I can count on Janet to support the difficult decision I have to make. Marsha and Greg are long-time collaborators who trust each other completely and who share a commitment to the foundations of education. However, it is clear that they no longer trust me and they are moving other faculty and staff in the same direction, particularly Sandra, the advisor who has now become quite vocal about my imminent decision. As the word gets out, anxiety is likely to be heightened and the faculty might find itself edging toward chaos.

Step 4: What do I know for certain? What do I still need to know?
Given how volatile this situation could potentially become, I think a Certainty Matrix will help me sort out how I can use what I already know to manage the uncertainties that lie ahead.

Step 5: What are my next steps?
Now that I have completed my relationship map and the Certainty Matrix, I can easily see what I need to do. Although I have no choice about cutting the courses, I need to keep in mind that this action will have an enormous effect on the faculty and their feelings about how their work is valued by the university. I also need to think about how I can minimize damage to relationships among faculty and staff and in particular, what effect these course cuts will have on trust in the faculty. I am aware that trust in me has

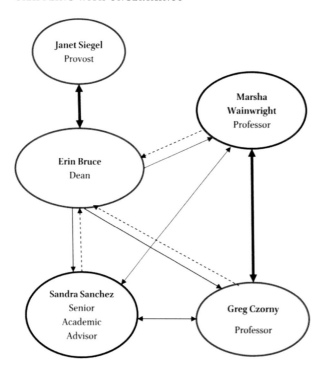

FIGURE 4.3 *Erin's relationship map (Dropping Enrolments)*

already been eroded so I will need to focus on how I can repair relationships with people who feel that I have betrayed them. I feel we are on the edge of chaos and it will be no small task to restore the equilibrium people need to work effectively together.

First, I will need to acknowledge publicly that I am going back on my word since I promised not to cut courses. I will need to remind the faculty and staff that sometimes, circumstances change and that we all need to adapt when that happens. Second, I will need to lead a dialogue with both faculty and staff to examine the question of course cuts more deeply. I need to make sure that all faculty and staff see the actual enrolment figures from the past 10 years so they are working with the same information that I have. I am going to have to remind faculty and staff that since there are few avenues for a university to balance its budget, that Deans are expected to cut courses when there is a financial shortfall. Third, I will need to acknowledge that cutting courses means that this will present difficulties if others are expected to "shoehorn" some of the content from the foundations courses into their existing curricula. Finally, I will need to assure faculty and staff that although some people may find that their duties will have changed, no one will lose their job and every effort will be

TABLE 4.3 *Erin's Certainty Matrix (Dropping Enrolments)*

	Certainties	Uncertainties
Warranted	*I know...* – that Marsha and Greg (among others) feel betrayed – that we can't continue to offer foundations courses if the faculty is losing money on them – that Sandra is concerned about the changes in staffing and is talking to others and the union about it – that I have the support of the Provost if I cut these courses – I am heading into a tumultuous time in which others' trust in me will be sorely tested	*I don't know...* – if Marsha and Greg will ever forgive me for the decision I am about to make – if we will ever be able to resurrect these courses – to what degree foundations courses are actually valued by the rest of the faculty
Unwarranted	*I think I know...* – how I might try to rebuild trust – how the rest of the support staff will be feeling if Sandra continues to raise concerns – what Janet will say if I tell her about the push-back I am seeing – how undergraduate students will react to this decision – how faculty will respond if they are expected to fold in foundations content into their courses	*I ought to know...* – if Sandra will be able to mobilize her union against the decisions I am about to make – where foundations content may be covered in other existing courses – the impact of this decision for current and future graduate students

made to support them during the transition. It may be difficult to swallow but I will point out that periods of uncertainty like this, while challenging, often afford surprising opportunities.

You know, it's amazing. The 5-step sensemaking approach may look really simple, but as you go through the steps, you realize there is nothing simple about it because the parts are moving all the time. (Superintendent)

Now that we have modeled the 5-step sensemaking approach for three scenarios, including answering the questions, drawing a relationship map, and completing the Certainty Matrix, we offer you an opportunity to engage in this sensemaking approach on your own. In the next chapter, we present a bank of scenarios for you to practice your skills in navigating complex problems. These scenarios feature principals, superintendents, and deans but the dilemmas could occur in any educational setting. Like the superintendent just quoted, we have no doubt you will find that the 5-step sensemaking approach is a valuable approach which becomes more intuitive with practice. No matter what uncertainties lay ahead for you, we think this approach can serve as a trusted compass.

CHAPTER 5

Responding to Cases of Uncertainty

This chapter includes 9 scenarios drawn from actual situations in which educational leaders, operating in different milieus, face a variety of complex problems. We invite readers to use these to practise using the 5-step sensemaking approach. As you read the scenarios, try to take the perspective of the educational leader who must manage the dilemma and apply this approach to come to a deeper understanding of the situation. Once you have mapped out the relationships and identified the warranted and unwarranted certainties and uncertainties, consider possible courses of action and what the impact of these might be on the networks, norms, and trust in the institution. It is important to remember that any of these dilemmas might occur in any setting and indeed, we have changed some of the settings and roles of the educational leaders in the interests of maintaining the anonymity of the participants.

1   Walking into a Minefield

Darlene Malloy had been a successful principal with a very good reputation in a large urban school district. However, when her husband's company downsized their operations, he was offered a transfer to another city that he couldn't refuse. Darlene reluctantly resigned from her "dream job" and relocated with her husband. She hoped that her years of administrative experience would stand her in good stead once she found another position. Being realistic, she also knew no matter what position she managed to find, it would take time to build new networks in which she was well-regarded as the one she was leaving.

Fortunately, it wasn't long before Darlene landed a new administrative position in a school district that was a lot like the one she had left. She was hired as a principal of a high school in an upwardly-mobile part of the city, in no small measure because of the connection she had made with the superintendent, Fraser Grant. A year ago, the two had met at a national advanced leadership convention when they were both on the same panel and soon after, they realized that they were kindred spirits. They remained in touch and often consulted each other when they had personal or professional problems. Fraser was delighted when her

© KONINKLIJKE BRILL NV, LEIDEN, 2018 | DOI 10.1163/9789004368484_005

application for a position in his district came up and he quickly hired her. He looked forward to having such a qualified administrator on his staff and someone he knew he could trust completely.

In his excitement about hiring Darlene and without any forethought, Fraser mentioned to union leaders, Joanie Patterson and Brent Cardwell that he was looking forward to some positive changes to staffing in the near future. He was proud of the fact that he had been able to "snag" a new principal with a national reputation who he had intended to place at Westbury High School. Joanie and Brent looked at each other in disbelief because as far as they knew, there was no vacant position at that school. Did this mean that their colleague, Brenda Murdoch was going to be out of a job and was she aware of this? They were outraged to find that someone from outside the system had been given preferential treatment. Before long, word spread throughout the membership that Brenda had been unceremoniously transferred to another school in the district and that Darlene would be arriving within the week. Resentment was running high. Within a few days, Fraser was shocked to find a notice of grievance on his desk. Although he was fairly certain that there were no grounds for the grievance, he was saddened that Darlene would be starting her career in the district on such a sour note.

A week later, when Darlene arrived to take up her position, Fraser was waiting for her at the door of Westbury High. She could tell from his body language that something was amiss. As Fraser escorted her to her new office, she braced herself for what she instinctively knew would be a difficult conversation. Within a few minutes, she realized that she was walking into a minefield and that she was going to have to tread very carefully.

2   Under the Bus

Hannah Farnsworth was an assistant superintendent with five years' experience as an administrator in a mid-sized, suburban school district. She worked closely with her superintendent, James Norris-Rogers, and Ron Liebowitz, the other assistant superintendent, as well as the consultants on the senior leadership team. Although the team generally seemed to work well together, Hannah and Ron were becoming increasingly frustrated with Deanna Tranquata, the English Language Arts consultant. Deanna was proving to be very challenging colleague as she was reluctant to share what she was doing with the teachers in the district's schools and she didn't accept constructive feedback very well. On top of that, she had a habit of distorting the facts so that she would always end up, "smelling like roses" no matter how difficult the situation. Her special bond with James didn't help matters either. James and Deanna had worked very closely for many years in another school district and there was some suggestion that their friendship had even been romantic at one time. The result was that neither Hannah nor Ron nor any of the other members of the leadership team felt they could be open with James about the problems they were experiencing with Deanna.

These concerns came to a head one day when the Board office received a phone call that would turn the entire school district office upside down. The caller accused Deanna of mistreating teachers who she was supposed to be supporting, yelling at them, and admonishing them in front of their colleagues. The source, who insisted on anonymity, claimed to represent a group of teachers in the district who were fed up with her behaviour. She ended the call with the threat that this group was ready to go to the union to make a complaint and that no matter what else happened, they expected that Deanna would be released from her duties as consultant immediately, pending a formal review.

As James listened to the recorded call, he wasn't sure just how seriously he needed to take it since he had never seen anything like this kind of behaviour in Deanna and he had never heard any complaints about her. He called Deanna into his office and asked her what she made of the allegations. Much to his surprise, she immediately became defensive, blamed the problem on the teachers, and even accused Hannah and Ron of being to blame. Deanna claimed that they provided little direction in their roles as assistant superintendents, kept her in the dark on district initiatives, and were generally disrespectful towards her. He was troubled by Deanna's complete lack of ownership and the way she had denigrated Ron and Hannah, who he knew to be highly able and thoroughly professional.

Once James heard the claims that Deanna was making, he realized that he had a bigger problem on his hands than he first thought. He immediately asked Hannah and Ron to join him in the conference room to brief them on the substance of the call and get their reactions to what Deanna had said. As he recounted his interview with Deanna to his assistant superintendents, James could see mounting disbelief in their eyes as they realized that their "colleague" had just thrown them under the bus. Although James wasn't certain what he would do next, he was suddenly very sure that what he thought was a well-functioning leadership team was anything but.

3   No Winners

Julia Drayton had been the dean of education at a small undergraduate college for five years after spending almost six years as an associate dean in the same institution. If not well-loved, she liked to think that she was well-respected by most of her colleagues and was seen to be an advocate for them and the work they did. However, she was aware that the series of college-wide initiatives designed to achieve institutional efficiencies was beginning to affect the way that faculty members regarded all of the administration, including her. What started as grumbling about the changes became more strident claims that the college was saving money on the backs of its faculty members. Even Margaret Thibodaux, who had been Julia's closest friend in the faculty, became increasingly vocal and angry about the way the faculty's academic work was being devalued. It was not long before other faculty members joined her, voicing their discontent about the way the administration was off-loading extra administrative tasks without additional compensation. Julia began to dread faculty meetings, which became increasingly contentious, emotional, and focused on complaints instead of the real work of the faculty.

As the collective agreement between the college and its 500 faculty members was set to expire, Julia had no doubt that growing resentment about working under the new "corporate agenda" was going to be a major issue. Sure enough, Stan Russo, head of the faculty union, and no friend of the administration, decided that enough was enough – it was time for faculty members to air their grievances. After a frustrating and protracted period of bargaining, negotiations ultimately broke down and strike action could no longer be averted. The labor disruption lasted for four weeks and though a settlement was ultimately reached between the college and the faculty union, it was widely acknowledged that there had been no winners.

Unfortunately, most of the faculty members who had gone on strike believed that nothing significant had been achieved and their colleagues, who had continued to teach, believed that a strike in the middle of term had been misguided and unfair to the students. Indeed, students were visibly frustrated by the interruption to their schedules and resentful about the days that they now had to make up to meet their professional certification requirements. Some made it very clear that they no longer regarded their professors with the same esteem as they had before the disruption.

As expected, the post-strike period was a difficult one – tension was palpable and hard feelings between those who had walked the picket line and those who didn't appeared to be almost insurmountable. However, Julia knew that her first priority would have to be helping the faculty heal the wounds the strike had left behind. As she looked ahead, she wondered how she could possibly repair the trust that had been so badly broken.

4   Who's at Risk?

Matthew Robinson was the principal of a middle school with a strong reputation in one of the leafy neighborhoods of a large urban centre. He worked closely with his vice-principal, Anne Starling with whom he had built a strong bond over the past five years. They had both just survived a very difficult year during which one of their teachers was dismissed due to professional misconduct. As a result of that case and a few others, their school district had moved to a much more formalized teacher evaluation system for teachers at risk. This would be the year that it would be tested out and Matthew and Anne both knew who was likely to be the first person of concern.

Silas Goffman was the school's longest-serving science teacher. Although he was very knowledgeable in his field, he had always had difficulty building relationships with students and consequently, classroom management had been a perennial problem. Matthew had worked intensively with him since he had come to the school and the two of them had developed a growing respect for one another. However, improvement had been minimal. Because families tended to stay in the neighborhood from one generation to the next, many of the students that Silas had taught in the past were now the parents of his current students. Predictably, very few of them had anything positive to say about him. In fact, with every passing year, Matthew and Anne could feel increasing pressure from parents to force Silas to retire or to transfer him to another school. Now that they had to implement the new teacher evaluation system, Matthew and Anne knew that they couldn't avoid "the Silas problem" any longer.

At about the same time that Matthew and Anne came to this conclusion, they received a phone call from a parent, Sherry Drysdale, whose son, Cooper, was in Silas's Grade 8 science class. According to Cooper, Silas had thrown a tennis ball at his head when he wasn't able to answer what Silas thought was a relatively simple question. Cooper admitted that without thinking, he had hurled the ball back at Silas breaking his glasses in the process. Before they knew it, mayhem had broken out in the classroom. Upon hearing the noise from down the hall, Faye Littlechild, one of Silas's teaching partners, intervened to calm things down. After being briefed by Faye, Matthew called Cooper's mother to tell her that he would look into the matter and speak to both Silas and Cooper immediately.

Unfortunately, his attempt to have those conversations was temporarily thwarted when he saw a small delegation of teachers, all members of Silas's teaching team, gathering outside his office. He was pretty sure what was on their minds. Faye spoke first and made the case that the situation had reached a tipping point – something had to be done about Silas. Not only was the disruption from his classroom having a negative effect on his students, but on *their* students as well. Later that day, Matthew and Anne met in Matthew's office. Matthew knew that in spite of his fondness for Silas, he would not only have to address what just happened but also what the future held for Silas at the school.

5   All Fired Up

Evelyn Shore was the chief superintendent of a sprawling, urban school district in a large metropolitan area on the west coast. She was responsible for over 100 schools and with that, over 300 school-based administrators. Most of those administrators were effective communicators who worked hard at establishing norms, networks and trust within their respective communities.

However, Evelyn mused, there were always at least 5% of those administrators who took 95% of her time. One of these was Frank Allen, a late career administrator. Frank was the principal of Harold Cardinal Middle School (HCMS) in one of the more affluent areas and was unfortunately, not among the most effective administrators in the district.

Although he was a fine human being, Evelyn had come to learn that he avoided difficult situations and when confronted with people who disagreed with his views had a tendency to become passive aggressive. Evelyn had come to his aid on more than one occasion because of his poor relationships with parents.

Such was the recent case with Tara Syme, one of HCMS's most vocal parents who had an opinion on almost everything. Tara was a long-time resident of the area with high expectations for everyone, especially school officials. Evelyn had heard her speak out often at school and district meetings on a variety of issues. Currently, Tara was most concerned about the lack of discipline in the school, the outdated physical education equipment, and the low academic standards. Because she was so outspoken and persuasive, she was able to get other parents fired up about the quality of education that their children were receiving. She went as far as encouraging her friends to talk to the educational assistants in the school to try to get insider information. Furthermore, some of teachers were telling Frank that Tara Syme and her group were spreading damaging stories about the school that wouldn't be good for any of their reputations.

When Evelyn heard that things were spiraling out of control yet again, she decided to meet with Frank to discuss the escalating situation. To her dismay, he seemed unmoved by the parents' concerns and unyielding when it came to Tara. There was no love lost between Tara and Frank and he was determined not to give into her attempts to micromanage the school.

Evelyn could quickly see that any efforts to bring Frank on side and work with him to address the parents' concerns would be futile. However, she was convinced that parents needed to know that the school and the district took their concerns seriously so she decided to hold a community meeting in which parents' concerns could be aired. Evelyn knew that calling this kind of meeting could backfire because although Frank was clearly part of the problem, she knew that it would be no simple matter to put out the fire that Tara had started.

No matter what happened at the meeting, it was abundantly clear that Frank needed a fresh start at another school. Although removing Frank might reset the school's balance in the short term, it didn't answer the question about what to do with Frank in the long-term. For that matter, it didn't address the concerns of the parents either. Looking ahead, she knew for sure that she would continue spending more time with Frank than she wanted to and that she still had a fire to put out!

6   Who Stands to Benefit?

Cliff Bennett was the dean of a faculty of education at a large research
intensive university that prided itself on being one of the top 10
universities in North America. With 250 full-time faculty members, it was
one of the largest faculties of its kind and one of the most productive.
Faculty members were expected to teach, conduct research, and
provide service to the faculty, the university and the wider educational
community. These expectations were the same criteria used to judge
applications for tenure and promotion. However, there was a perception,
at least among a vocal few, that treating everyone the same was an
outrage. In their opinion, assigned duties should be more differentiated
allowing 'serious' researchers to be exempt from service and to have a
much lighter teaching load.

No one was making the case louder than Felicity Mulholland who
had just landed a multi-year external grant worth millions of dollars.
Recently, Felicity had teamed up with Brian Frost and Joanna Magnusson
who were just as disgruntled as she was about the emphasis on university
and community service. Collectively, the three of them were bringing
in more research dollars than the rest of the Faculty combined. On the
other hand, they each realized that the amount of service that they had
performed would not warrant promotion to Full Professor which each of
them had applied for earlier that year.

Given the circumstances, Cliff should not have been surprised
when, at a Faculty Council meeting, Felicity rose with her motion to
establish a process for revising the Faculty's Promotion Guidelines and
to differentiate requirements. As soon as the motion was read, Cliff
immediately found it difficult to maintain order because so many people
wanted to speak to the motion. Although Cliff could see merit in the
idea of differentiation and had actually been looking into the possibility
with other faculties, this was not the way he hoped to introduce this
idea. Instead, there were faculty members publicly accusing the three of
being high-handed and interested only in their own career ambitions.
Many of these same people saw service as an integral part of their roles
and were offended by the suggestion that some of their colleagues should
be exempt in any way. With emotions running high, Cliff suggested that
they table the motion until the next meeting so that people could have
the time to prepare written submissions that could be read and carefully
considered before the next meeting was called. Although there was

further heated discussion, most people realized that Cliff's suggestion was reasonable except for Felicity, Brian and Joanna whose faces were red with anger. They had come to the meeting on a mission. They needed the motion to be passed and passed now or there wouldn't be enough time for them to benefit personally by the changes they were advocating. Although many people could support the notion of differentiation, the fact that these three brought it forward in the year that they were applying for promotion, was simply repugnant. As the meeting wrapped up, Cliff wondered how he could balance the merit of the proposal against what was clearly self-interest on the part of Felicity, Brian and Joanna. Even more concerning was the rift that he saw widening in the Faculty – how was he going to avoid a two-tiered faculty in which some people were perceived to have special dispensations?

7   Jumping the Gun

Patrick Delaney was a principal at Oakdale School which was situated in a largely rural area. He was generally well-liked and after only 2 ½ years at the school, had already galvanized the school staff around some major initiatives. In fact, he had reached out to parents in new and engaging ways. Parents now played a major role in working with the school staff to decide on school-wide initiatives and even set the criteria for hiring new teachers. Patrick was particularly pleased that parents had raised enough money to help the school invest in new technologies, including hallway cameras to reduce incidents of bullying. That is why he was so disappointed when a father of one of the students, Richard Mueller reported that his son, Peter, had complained that his teacher, Linda Bryant, had bullied him. Linda's reputation in the school was exemplary; in fact, it was so strong that she was a mentor to many of the school's new teachers. Patrick was pretty sure who he could trust, but he assured Mr. Mueller that he would look into the matter and get back to him shortly. Although he knew he needed to contact Linda immediately, he was too pressed for time to see her. He was heading out of town on a two–day conference where he was the keynote speaker. With minutes left before he had to leave for the airport, all he had time to do was jot a quick note about the incident to Virginia Potter, the acting principal.

With Patrick in transit and out of contact, Virginia decided to find out as much as she could about the situation by talking to Linda. Virginia had long admired Linda and wanted to support her in any way possible. She could see that Linda was beginning to worry about damage to her reputation and was anxious to put this behind her immediately. They conferred with some of their other trusted colleagues and on their suggestion, contacted the local union representative, Gord Blochner. After a few conversations with him, Virginia was convinced that the situation could not wait until Patrick got back and that she and Linda would have to handle the situation on their own.

Meanwhile, Patrick had, in fact, been taking care of the situation. On the plane, he reviewed the video footage of the incident that showed that Linda was merely guiding Peter in the right direction, not physically bullying him as Peter had claimed. When Patrick put down the phone, after speaking to Peter's father, he was satisfied that there was no need for further action. Upon his return, Patrick was quick to tell Linda that he had taken care of the situation. Only then did he learn that Virginia and Linda had taken matters into their own hands while he was away. As a result, a relatively minor, private incident had become a much more serious and public matter.

Patrick was disappointed to hear that Virginia and Linda had involved others on staff by discussing the issue with them and that the teachers' union was now involved. He wasn't sure what his next steps would be but clearly, he needed to give some thought to how things had gotten so out of control in his absence and what he would need to do to clean up the mess.

8   Going Rogue

Greg Sawchuk was the superintendent of a rapidly growing, rural, school district. He was especially proud of his role in developing the new state-of-the-art high school campus, a sprawling, three-acre facility that was capable of accommodating 2,000 students. He had been pleased to have Alistair Norfolk join the senior leadership team at the school as campus administrator last year because he had strong interpersonal skills and extensive experience as a facilities manager in the district. Greg came to rely on him to work closely with the contractors and assist him in staying on top of the myriad of details that such an extensive building project entailed. However, lately, Greg found himself wondering whether the pressures of managing such a large facility had been too much for Alistair. People at the high school and even at the Board Office were beginning to notice that Alistair had become uncharacteristically short-tempered and unpredictable of late.

Greg's concerns came to a head when, late in December, he discovered that one of the teachers in the school, Merv St. Pierre, was accusing Alistair of harassment. Apparently, Alistair had taken to dropping in on Merv's classes and chatting with him afterwards. During one of these conversations, Merv jokingly asked whether Alistair was evaluating his teaching and questioned why, as a campus administrator, he was taking on this role. Alistair became furious with Merv for questioning his authority and stomped out of his classroom. On the advice of staff officers from the local teachers' federation, Merv agreed to meet with Alistair formally with a union representative at his side to discuss the situation. However, when Alistair e-mailed him the day before they were to meet and instructed him to bring five days of lesson plans with him or face suspension, Merv had had enough. He called his principal, Evan Sreenivassan to apprise him of the situation and Evan immediately contacted Greg.

Greg was flabbergasted when Evan told him what Alistair had done. As far as Greg was concerned, this was completely out of character for Alistair. Besides everyone knew that teacher evaluation was the purview of principals and vice-principals and that district policy invested superintendents alone with the authority to suspend teachers. Evan and Greg met with Merv that afternoon and reassured him that he was in no danger of "suspension" and they promised Merv that Alistair would not be involved in teacher evaluation.

Greg was now concerned about Alistair's mental health. Cautiously, he approached him and asked if they could meet to talk about what had happened with Merv. To his surprise and dismay, Alistair replied, "Sure, we can meet but I'm bringing my lawyer and I'm going to record everything you say." As Greg began to dig deeper, he learned from Evan that he and his three vice-principals had been tormented by Alistair's increasingly authoritarian behaviour for months. Greg didn't have to ask why they had not told him. With a sinking feeling, he knew that his preoccupation with overseeing the completion of the campus had essentially taken him out of the equation. In the meantime, the situation had deteriorated so badly that two of the vice-principals were seriously considering leaving the district. Greg realized that while he wasn't looking, Alistair had pushed the school leadership to the edge of chaos and it was now going to take a great deal of work to put it back on an even keel.

9   The Great Professor

Barbara Fenwick had been the dean of education at a small faculty of education in a primarily undergraduate university for almost three years. As a superintendent for the previous eight years and a school principal for almost fifteen years before that, she had faced her fair share of human resource challenges. The one that kept her up at night these days was Marina Umsbrutt – the faculty bully. Professor Umsbrutt was a world-renowned scholar in educational administration, had published countless books and articles in peer-reviewed journals, and was very much in demand as a speaker at conferences around the world. Her standing not only enhanced the credibility of the faculty, but also that of the university. Unfortunately, her glowing reputation resided entirely *outside* the walls of the university, while *inside*, it was far from rosy.

Marina was exceedingly difficult to get along with, particularly if she didn't get what she wanted or expected from Barbara, the associate deans, or her department head. She seemed to like to throw her weight around, constantly demanding additional resources and special recognition. She insisted that the rules be bent for her graduate students whenever they missed deadlines or wanted to take courses outside their programs. Barbara thought, more than once, that Marina was incapable of considering anyone else's needs or feelings and that she was acting as if the faculty was her private academic playground. When Marina's unreasonable demands were refused, as they often had to be, she vented her displeasure on the support staff and fired off angry emails to the rest of the faculty and was quick to file grievances with the faculty association.

As a result of her volatile and aggressive behaviour within the faculty, Marina had very few supporters, except for two ambitious young faculty members, Darren Finnbogan and Marjorie Cullen. They admired her work and saw her behaviour as a model for how to get ahead in the academic world. Everyone else simply steered clear of "The Great Professor" preferring to ignore the chaos that swirled around her. Unfortunately, support staff were unable to avoid Marina's all too frequent tirades.

The latest incident made Barbara realize that she would have to do something soon. Marina had not only upset Frances Bay, the faculty admissions clerk, but also presented Barbara with a real dilemma. Apparently, Marina had met a professor on one of her many trips abroad who had hosted her and been generous with his hospitality. Now his son was looking for a graduate program and was expecting Marina to pull whatever strings necessary and she had assured him that she would make it happen. In fact, Marina had pressured Frances to the point of tears to fast track his admission and overlook the usual eligibility requirements. When Frances finally approached Barbara with Marina's demands, she knew that she would need to take "the bully by the horns" but she also knew that this would be a battle with "casualties" and that whatever she did or said, a grievance would not be far behind.

Index

Printed in the United States
By Bookmasters